PRAISE FOR

GRUMPY MOM TAKES A HOLIDAY

Filled with grace, hope, and practical ways forward for every momma, *Grumpy Mom Takes a Holiday* is a necessary read for anyone struggling to find refreshment and abundance in the everyday moments of motherhood. Discover how to take a holiday from being Grumpy Mom and turn to God's truth about who you are.

CANDACE CAMERON BURE
Actress and *New York Times* bestselling author

Val has been discipling women, moms, and our generation with her words and her products for years—and this book just continues that good work. She uses the same gifts of vulnerability and honest truth to serve us—her readers—and she'll leave you encouraged and spurred on to embrace joy right where you're at.

JESS CONNOLLY
Speaker; coauthor of *Wild and Free* and *Always Enough, Never Too Much*; author of *Dance Stand Run*

In a world that often coddles us in our #hotmessmom comfort, *Grumpy Mom Takes a Holiday* looks at joy in motherhood exactly how the Bible does: joy isn't a feeling; it's a choice. And the results of choosing joy extend far beyond merely living a happier life. As you travel through these chapters with your new friend Val, you'll definitely laugh. You'll probably cry. But most of all, you'll gain a godly determination to be the mom today you want your kids to remember tomorrow.

MICHELLE MYERS
Founder of she works HIS way and author of *Famous in Heaven and at Home*

Okay, fellow Grumpy Mom, Valerie does not shy away from the reality of yucky inner thoughts and motivations. On these pages, you will find a friend who understands the challenges of parenting little ones while living out your God-appointed ministries. She graciously invites you send "the grumps" packing and embrace a better, joy-filled way.

HEATHER MACFADYEN
Host of the *Don't Mom Alone* podcast

I am not a momma, but I *am* an advocate of community and the hope that can flourish within it. And if I have learned anything from my momma friends, it's that you can't do this thing alone, yet daily you find yourself feeling just that way at one time or another—alone. Valerie has a way of being able to see you in the trenches, grab your hand out of compassion, and gently pull you up with the truth "he's got this, he's got you, and he's got them." A community of mommas will gather around these pages and see hope flourish.

JENN JETT
Freedom fighter and dream defender; founder of The Well Studio and Camp Well

Yes, yes, yes! Can we please have more books like this? As a mom of three little girls ages three and under, I am determined to not be "that" mom—the one who is grumpy and always complaining about the little blessings I begged for. Instead, I choose joy. I choose to join Valerie on this vacation—a forever vacation—of finding the indescribable joy in motherhood. Thank you, Valerie, for making me laugh and cry, and most of all for reminding me of this high calling of motherhood and what a *joy* it can be if I decide not to be Grumpy Mom.

DR. ALY TAYLOR
Author, speaker, and reality star of TLC's *Rattled*

If you're a mom who has ever struggled with getting grumpy with your kids (quite possibly all of us!), then you're going to be encouraged and inspired by Valerie Woerner in *Grumpy Mom Takes a Holiday*. While she can relate to the very real challenges of motherhood, she also offers hope and action steps to help you find peace and joy in your amazing role as a mom.

LISA JACOBSON
Club31Women.com

After reading this book, you will be encouraged and empowered and feel a little less alone. This book will help replace the lies you might believe about yourself as a mom and offer a redemptive and refreshing perspective on motherhood. This book has held a mirror to my most vulnerable moments as a new mom and challenged me to turn my grumblings into gratitude. The truth-bomb reminders in the book will transform how you teach, care for, and respond to your children. As you read, you will be filled up with more grace, joy, and love for yourself and your littles.

AUDREY ROLOFF
Coauthor of *A Love Letter Life*, founder of Always More, and cofounder of Beating50Percent

In a culture that offers us a bazillion reasons to blame our kids for our stress and exhaustion, *Grumpy Mom Takes a Holiday* challenges readers to reconsider the blessing of motherhood. Val gently leads us to face this truth: we're not victims of our motherhood—we're victors as we surrender to God's Spirit. Pick up this book and rediscover the joy of being the mom God created you to be.

ASHERITAH CIUCIU
Founder of One Thing Alone Ministries and author of *Full: Food, Jesus, and the Battle for Satisfaction*

As moms living in a digital age with endless demands on our time, we need the hopeful message Val offers in *Grumpy Mom Takes a Holiday*. The "holiday" Val describes isn't the normal getaway we often desire. Instead, she offers us a better way of living and embracing our roles in motherhood by learning the gift of contentment right where God has placed us. Val's honesty will have you nodding your head as if you are sharing with a close friend over a cup of coffee. For every tired and overworked mom out there, this book will send you on your way with hope in your heart and joy in your step.

GRETCHEN SAFFLES
Writer and founder of Well-Watered Women

Grumpy Mom Takes a Holiday left me cheering out loud and filled with new peace with every turn of the page! This refreshing and actionable book delivers on its promise and more: I have found new joy in motherhood and in my faith, thanks to Val's insightful words. I couldn't put this book down!

LARA CASEY
Author of *Make It Happen* and *Cultivate*

GRUMPY

Say goodbye to

MOM

stressed, tired, and anxious,

TAKES A

and say hello to

HOLIDAY

renewed joy in motherhood

VALERIE WOERNER

TYNDALE
MOMENTUM®

The nonfiction imprint of
Tyndale House Publishers, Inc.

Visit Tyndale online at www.tyndale.com.

Visit Tyndale Momentum online at www.tyndalemomentum.com.

Visit the author online at www.valmariepaper.com.

TYNDALE, *Tyndale Momentum*, and Tyndale's quill logo are registered trademarks of Tyndale House Publishers, Inc. The Tyndale Momentum logo is a trademark of Tyndale House Publishers, Inc. Tyndale Momentum is the nonfiction imprint of Tyndale House Publishers, Inc., Carol Stream, Illinois.

Grumpy Mom Takes a Holiday: Say Goodbye to Stressed, Tired, and Anxious, and Say Hello to Renewed Joy in Motherhood

Designed by Julie Chen

Edited by Stephanie Rische

Published in association with Folio Literary Management, LLC, 630 9th Avenue, Suite 1101, New York, NY 10036.

For information about special discounts for bulk purchases, please contact Tyndale House Publishers at csresponse@tyndale.com, or call 1-800-323-9400.

ISBN 978-1-4964-3530-9

Printed in the United States of America

25	24	23	22	21	20	19
7	6	5	4	3	2	1

This book is dedicated to every momma
who's ready to show the world
what refreshed motherhood looks like.

CONTENTS

FOREWORD

THE FIRST CONVERSATION I had with Val happened over Voxer. If you've never heard of Voxer, it's basically a walkie-talkie app on your phone. I feel like Voxer is proof that Jesus loves moms. When you're having trouble adulting as a mom, you can escape to your bathroom, lock the door, and open up your Voxer app to talk to other moms who are hiding in *their* bathrooms.

I don't remember what my issue was the day Val reached out to me. I *do* remember how she started her message to me: "Jennifer, let me pray for you." And then she did just that. She prayed the most beautiful prayer. Her words gave me the peace and perspective I needed.

I tell you this because you need to know that Val is an intensely trustworthy guide, with the words you need to hear in this season of your life. Her heart beats like this: *Jesus ... Jesus ... Jesus.*

But this isn't some impossibly pious book by some impossibly pious woman. Yeah, she's the kind of friend who will pray for you. She's also the woman who will laugh at your jokes. She's the next-door neighbor you wish you had. Val is the kind of woman who would share her last piece of chocolate with you. (Well, I *thought* she would share her chocolate, but then I read chapter 6, "When They Cry, I Eat Chocolate." So the jury is still out on that one.)

Val is *definitely* the kind of woman who, if she came to your house today, wouldn't bat an eye at the Lego city that is experiencing urban sprawl on your living room floor. She wouldn't care that there's an Everest-sized mountain of laundry on your dining room table. And she would affirm your insistent belief that ketchup counts as a vegetable.

Val is the friend you will absolutely listen to, because she will get super honest with you first. That's my favorite kind of friend, and that's my favorite kind of writer. I don't have much tolerance for books written by people who are unwilling to disclose their own struggles while doling out advice like one of those annoying guys at shopping mall kiosks who have "just the product for you." Nope. Dot. Com.

What you'll get here is full transparency. You'll get to meet Grumpy Mom Val. And maybe that's how you will get honest enough to find your own Grumpy Mom Self. The thing is, we've got to drag Grumpy Mom out from behind the locked bathroom door and into the light before we can send her on an extended vacation to Siberia.

So yeah, Val might step on your toes a little bit while you're reading this book, but you'll survive. As I say to my own children: "But are you bleeding?"

Here's what else Val will do: she'll make you laugh when she reminds you that sometimes motherhood feels like all the shots are being called by the tiny dictators in your life. She'll make you sigh with relief when you realize you're not alone.

And get this—she'll actually help you send Grumpy Mom packing. Val doesn't just say a lot of nice words about some things. She gives doable action steps that even the busiest mom can handle.

And in the end, you'll feel confident that you can leave a lasting legacy of love for the littles in your home. That's what almost every mom I know worries about: the legacy we're leaving. We all harbor secret concerns that our kids will remember us as Grumpy Mom-zillas.

As Val gently reminds us, "The legacy we leave starts *inside* of us." And then she tells us that because of Jesus' love for us and for our kids, a lasting legacy is possible. That's exactly what I need to know as a mom: that Jesus loves this hot mess and that he will help me through this.

Just this morning, Val's message echoed in my heart when I was on the verge of losing my cool with one of my teenage daughters. She had overslept and was running late, and I was afraid we wouldn't get to the bus stop in time. I was about to snap, but then I took a deep breath and offered grace instead of harsh words. Turns out, she didn't miss the bus after all. In that moment, I was so relieved that I listened to Val's voice in my head and found my chill instead of blowing a gasket over the teenage equivalent of spilled milk.

Moms, let me tell you one more thing. You will love this whole book, but one of my very favorite parts comes at the end, so don't stop reading until you get there. Promise?

I read the final pages through tears as Val reminded me that we moms don't have to wait until nap time to find joy.

We don't have to wait until the kids are all grown up and gone to fulfill our callings.

We can have fulfillment right here, right now.

That's what awaits you—the kind of peace, joy, and fulfillment that you can find out in the light—on the other side of the bathroom door.

Jennifer Dukes Lee,
author of *It's All Under Control*
and *The Happiness Dare*

INTRODUCTION

I HAD VALID REASONS TO BE GRUMPY. Or so I told myself. The
past several weeks had been pushing all my mom buttons: my
workload was overwhelming; my younger daughter, Vana, was
teething; my older daughter, Vivi, was constantly whining; and
my husband, Tyler, kept coming home late from work. On top
of all that, the Louisiana summer made it too hot to function
outside. The world had handed me my scepter and crown and
made me Lady Grumpy Mom over all Woerner land and beyond.

My days consisted of walking around on pins and needles
waiting for (and dreading) the moment one of my two bundles
of joy would burst into tears or whines. When the house was
quiet—if they were giggling together or playing quietly in their
separate corners—instead of enjoying the moment of peace,
I braced myself to release Grumpy Mom as soon as I got orders
to pounce. It was as if I thought any bump in life demanded her
presence. And motherhood will certainly give you plenty of
bumps to test that theory if you let it.

So there I was, floundering through the witching hour and
waiting at the door like a puppy dog for my husband to come
home—not because I longed to enjoy his company, but because

I wanted to tap out and escape the circumstances I was convinced were stealing my joy.

We've all been there as moms, haven't we? We know, deep down, that our children are gifts and that we have so much to be grateful for. But discontentment sneaks into our hearts anyway, and we find ourselves huddled in the bathroom or in the closet, sulking about how hard it is to parent day in and day out. When we finally emerge, our kids know to stay out of Mom's way for a while. And if they don't? That's our cue to start yelling. Many times these aren't full-blown fits, just tense words with an underlying aggressive tone. In our hearts, we are longing for some sort of escape, preferably involving sunglasses, sand, and the sound of ocean waves.

Maybe you even feel a little guilty or ashamed for picking up this book in the first place—after all, you want to be marked by joy, and you long to be one of those moms who takes everything in stride. But the truth is, motherhood at any stage isn't easy. If Grumpy Mom lives at your house sometimes, you're in good company.

But the purpose of this book isn't just to commiserate over the hard stuff; the point is to discover together a better way. We don't have to resort to Grumpy Mom status, even when life gets busy or our kids misbehave or life doesn't go the way we hope it will. I think we know this to be true, but in our bustling homes, it's easy to neglect the quiet whisper reminding us that the Holy Spirit is at work within us and that we have the power to choose joy no matter what's happening around us.

The trigger for me that something needed to change in my perspective came on an otherwise ordinary day when I was tucking my then-three-year-old into bed. As I curled up beside her in her toddler bed under the fluffiest fleece flamingo blanket, I was feeling particularly grateful for her. And on that day, I actually thought to pass that information along.

"You make me smile so much, Vivi!" I said.

You should have seen the way she beamed. Her grin immediately spread wider than I had ever seen it. She said, "That makes me so happy to hear, momma!"

I reveled in the moment with her and treasured her cute little profile as she looked up at the ceiling and sang made-up songs for me. Then I kissed her good night and scurried off to tell my husband all about it. I loved that my joy could make her happy too.

But as I reveled in that special moment, I began to wonder why it had made such an impact on her. Was it really so earth shattering for her to see me smile? Why was she so surprised that she'd made me happy? Didn't that sentiment come across every day?

As I reflected on this scene, I finally made this admission to myself: *There's a slight chance I've been grumpier than I thought.* But where did Grumpy Mom come from? What stole my smiles without my knowledge? And why did I struggle endlessly to simply enjoy my life?

I couldn't let this go. And that meant it was time to do some digging, studying, praying, and introspective thinking. You know, just a fun Saturday night for a nerd like me. Over the following weeks, I came to what has been a life-changing realization: I didn't have to escape my life as a mom when things got chaotic to experience joy. It was time for me to stop playing the victim and take some ownership. I didn't need to take a holiday from my mom life; I needed to take a holiday from being Grumpy Mom. Of course, I would have preferred to banish her to some island for life, like Napoleon. But I knew that I wouldn't be able to get rid of Grumpy Mom permanently. This was a decision I'd have to make over and over again. And lucky for us, it doesn't take a permanent banishment of Grumpy Mom for us to experience radically refreshed motherhood.

Armed with a renewed fire in my belly to pursue the abundant life Jesus calls us to, I cranked up a worship playlist, diffused an essential oil (aptly named Joy), and threw back the curtains to let in that early morning (and I mean earrrrly morning) sunshine. As I did, I connected more dots: *joy is something we have to fight for.*

The tricky thing about our struggle is that it's not always obvious we're in a battle. We have an enemy who is cunning—he knows he doesn't have to make us awful; he can just flash some shiny objects in front of us to keep us distracted from God's big plan. When I think about the way the world sees motherhood, I start recognizing the shiny distractions.

The world's sentiments about motherhood may seem innocent at first glance:

1. Moms can't function without coffee.
2. A trip to Target with the kids rivals a day in prison.
3. Is it wine-thirty yet?
4. The only way moms can get a break is to hide out in the bathroom.
5. If you have a white couch, your child is bound to destroy it.

If you are reading this book, I'm guessing you have fallen for some of the world's lies about motherhood at some point. We've heard it all. Moms are tired. Moms are emotional. Moms are control freaks. Moms are terrible friends. The worst part is that we allow these things to become the dominant voice determining our thoughts and actions. But this doesn't have to be the end of our story. Romans 12:2 is about to become the anthem for anyone who wants to send Grumpy Mom on a holiday: "Do not conform to the pattern of this world, but be transformed by the renewing of your mind. Then you will be able to test and approve what God's will is—his good, pleasing and perfect will" (NIV). I love how *The Message* words this verse: "Don't become so well-adjusted to your culture that you fit into it without even thinking." *Without even thinking.* That's exactly the danger—that we accept the world's subpar clichéd version of motherhood without even realizing we could be living something better. It becomes second nature for us to stay in the pigeonhole the world puts us in. We think we have no choice but to live up to the stereotype of moms as worriers and hot messes.

The life we live is often far below what God has graciously gifted to us, and it should come as no surprise that *this* is when Grumpy Mom sneaks in. We spend our days focusing on the things of this world and end up living an insane life when the Lord has offered us abundance and soundness of mind. We have bought into an idea of "normal motherhood," which when you really think about it, is completely not normal.

- Do you feel totally overwhelmed when falling into bed?
- Are you consumed with worries about the future?
- Does your child's tantrum ruin the rest of your day?
- Are you preoccupied with schedules and to-do lists?
- Are you infinitely stressed about how you will get it all done?

If this is what motherhood is most days, then we are in need of a change. We need that transformed life Romans talks about. And I for one am ready to fight for it.

YOUR ESCAPE FROM GRUMPY-LAND

I wrote this book not because I have this all figured out, but out of my own experiences as a grumpy mom. I still have those explosive moments when I slam doors, discipline my kids apart from Jesus, throw myself a pity party, and eat the weight of my feelings in fancy chocolate.

I'm in the thick of motherhood right now. As my husband, Tyler, and I raise our two girls—Vivi, four, and Vana, two— I have plenty of chances to become Grumpy Mom. My naturally melancholy personality latches on to any reason to be unhappy with my life, no matter how great it actually is. But somehow the Lord is in the process of grabbing hold of my weary heart and helping me to latch on to hope instead. This hope is available to all of us—hope that we don't have to stay stuck in Grumpy-land, with no possibility of change, because God invites us to trade in the world's definition of motherhood for his truth. That simple truth has life-changing implications.

In the chapters ahead, we will combat the lies we moms tend to believe and look at ways to renew our minds. You'll find twenty misconceptions about motherhood, divided into five hope-filled sections: surrender, replenish, develop, connect, and thrive. We'll start with surrendering a few specific misconceptions that we tend to hold on to tighter than my youngest daughter holds on to her paci. Next, we'll learn where we can go to fuel up for the journey ahead. Then we'll develop a few key spiritual muscles, which will enable real transformation to happen. After that, we'll look at how a change in our perspectives can revolutionize our relationships. Lastly, we'll look at ways we can go beyond simply getting rid of grumpy and move toward thriving instead.

You can read through the book as a whole, or you can jump

to the areas that are obvious triggers for Grumpy Mom to visit your house.

My promise to you is that as you start replacing what the world tells us about motherhood with what God says, it will change your disposition and your view of motherhood.

The temptations to lose hope and become discouraged will still come up (there's no changing that!), but you'll be equipped to send Grumpy Mom packing before she gets too comfortable taking up residence in your heart. You'll be able to choose a more hopeful approach, which means more joy and more energy in motherhood. We can experience something far better than what this world has to offer. We can show patience and grace to our kids in a way that points them to Jesus. We can feel delight as God uses and refines us. And maybe we can eat just enough chocolate to feel pure enjoyment over life's little pleasures instead of enough to get a bellyful of regret.

Here's my mission for all the discouraged and weary moms: to ensure that our kids will remember us as mommas with smiles on our faces—not because we're fake or phony, but because we're being continuously renewed by truth. They'll see us as moms who have all the same issues and rough days as everyone else but who take our thoughts captive, lay them at the feet of Jesus, and exchange them for his truth. Then those thoughts can unleash the good life, which isn't just on some distant beach but is right here in front of us.

Momma, I hope this book will refresh your soul like a much-needed vacation, even if in reality you are reading this from a dimly lit closet, hiding from your kids.

SPRING 2019

PART ONE

SURRENDER

Chapter 1

EMOJI OVERLOAD

Say Hello to Steady Emotions

A FEW SUMMERS AGO, my family and I found ourselves bunked up at my sister's house for several days during a flood that destroyed a good chunk of South Louisiana. On the third day of being cooped up with a toddler with no toys and a three-month-old with only a few diapers left, we started getting news that the waters were rising. So was my blood pressure. Being the intro-est introvert you will ever meet, I was going crazy not having my usual moments of the day to myself.

I don't remember what put the wheels in motion, but my husband said something, and I went ballistic. I could not be calmed down. And the more my husband and then my sister tried to calm me down, the more I insisted that I was being totally calm and rational.

In hindsight?

I. Was. Not.

So Tyler and I hashed it out awkwardly in the driveway in front of some storm do-gooders who had decided to pick up trash about three feet from our heated conversation. Eventually this truth came out: my husband thought I was very up and down. One minute I was sharing some sage advice, telling women on Instagram how I find peace or joy, and the next minute I was flipping out. What I *heard* my husband say was that he thought I was a phony. Cue more tears.

The rest of that week (after the waters receded enough for us to get home without needing a lifeboat), I thought a lot about this conversation. I hated that I could be so Spirit filled one minute and so rage filled the next. Every moment God was at work in me felt incredibly real. But there was no question about it, those sweet moments were often all too short.

At the time, I *happened* (that's Southern Baptist for "God orchestrated") to be reading *Emotionally Healthy Spirituality* by Peter Scazzero. As I learned just how important it is to care for our emotions as part of our spiritual health, it struck me for the first time how little attention I gave to my emotional health. Sure, I had Bible reading and prayer in my holy rotation of daily activities, but tending to my emotional health? What for?

Scazzero says, "We know we have found our balance when we are so deeply rooted in God that our activity is marked by the peaceful, joyful, rich quality of our contemplation."[1] The rich quality of our contemplation? You are chuckling, right? Who has time for that?

What I've learned from a few decades of "lessons," we'll call them, is that we're more willing to work on problem areas when things get bad enough. Maybe right now you are feeling desperate and drained of every possible tear. Your voice is hoarse from yelling (I've been there), and your body is brittle (I've been there, too). If that's where you find yourself, I don't have to convince you that rich contemplation is worth it. You're all in. But if you don't think emotions affect your life that much right now, you might be tempted to skip this chapter, thinking you have bigger fish to fry. But no matter where you are on the emotional spectrum, this is a good place for all of us to start.

If we are going to tackle our inner Grumpy Mom to the floor, we have to start by first addressing the assumption that all moms are overly emotional. Swarming around us is the idea that women and, even more so, moms are just an utter mess of feelings. We're ticking time bombs, and our kids have to do dance moves around the activation switch. These thoughts are enough to make even a pretty stable momma feel on edge.

There's nothing wrong with emotions—in fact, the ability to feel is a gift from God. But the world would lead us to believe that instead of having control over our emotions, we are ruled by them. At times I have felt utterly unstable emotionally, and I think this cultural misconception is what planted the idea in the first place. Somehow I crossed over from feeling a little scattered and stressed to one tantrum (my girls', not mine) away from an all-out breakdown.

When we found out our second child was going to be a girl, one of my first reactions was to feel bad for my husband. Not because he'd miss out on all the father-son things, but because our house would be wall-to-wall tears or giggles, always cranked to an eleven in either direction. I wasn't sure he could handle the emotions of three females.

This breaks my heart a little. The assumption that girls can't process their emotions in a healthy way is all around us, and it's wreaking havoc on us and our daughters. But here's some hope for us: we *can* process emotions in a healthy way. We aren't limited to the world's labels, because our God is not limited by anything.

So embrace your heart, fragile as it may be, and let's talk about a better mind-set when it comes to processing our emotions.

GET ME OFF THIS THING

Emotions were on my mind so much during my second pregnancy. Everywhere I turned, the topic seemed to come up—in webinars, in books, and in sermons. Then, three weeks before I gave birth to Vana, my sister got married, and less than twelve hours after I cried myself down the aisle as matron of honor, my cousin passed away unexpectedly and I bawled again, this time on my parents' porch. The range of emotions I experienced in the weeks prior to and after Vana's birth sent me on a roller coaster and all but consumed me. Pregnancy was the ultimate honesty filter. There was no possible way to suppress what I was feeling as I had attempted to do in the past. (I can say from experience that either extreme—stuffing the emotions or letting them fly all over the place—can be equally as dangerous.) It was during this time that I learned the driving power of emotions—and how clueless I was in dealing with them.

One of the biggest realizations that came to me from the sermons and books I read (okay, mostly the movie *Inside Out*) is that emotions are actually good indicators that we should take a deeper look inward. But we should manage them instead of letting them dictate our lives.

Does life sometimes feel like a roller coaster? Do you wake

up wondering if it's going to be a good day or a bad day based on whether your baby misses his nap or your toddler has a bad day herself? It's exhausting, isn't it? Living this way is the definition of survival mode. We hold on for dear life and let our emotions buck us around like a wild stallion. If you have never had a season where your emotions called the shots in your life, I tip my hat to you, ma'am. For the rest of us, this is totally normal, and dare I say, everyday life.

If you're ready to hop off the stallion, would you take a moment to picture another reality with me? Before your feet hit the floor in the morning, you lie in bed, look up at the ceiling, and praise Jesus for a new day. You tell him that you are excited to see what he has planned and that you are choosing right now to obey his lead instead of the leading of your emotions. Your heart isn't racing as you walk toward the dark abyss of a day full of unknowns. You know exactly what's to come—not the actual circumstances, but who you will be in the midst of them. Sure, one of your kids may barge into your room screaming for breakfast, but you hold out your hand and notice something new. It's steady like a Marine. Although you still can't predict what your kids will do, your heart is no longer set to the temperature of your circumstances. It's set to God's truth: that he is with you always, that he loves you, that his plan is better than anything you could come up with on your own. These truths trump anything the world will throw your way today, and as a result, you're calm and at peace.

We don't have to be slaves to the version of motherhood we see in all the movies: the mom who has stress in her life (shocker!) and then unleashes a storm of emotions on her kids, her spouse, and anyone else within earshot. This depiction of motherhood isn't just a fictionalized Hollywood version either.

We've seen it at Target, too—the mom who has stress in her life (in the form of a toddler) and starts yelling and slapping her kid and telling them to be quiet and stop hitting. We have bought into the lie that this is normal. Yes, tantrums in Target are normal. (And by this I mean that tantrums in Target are normal . . . for kids.) But we can flip the script when it comes to the way we respond.

CRYING OVER SPILLED MILK

Have you ever been scared of your kids? Not scared *for* them, but scared that they'll dictate how your day will turn out? I've been there, and it's utterly exhausting. And isn't this part of the reason we get so frustrated with them sometimes—because they have single-handedly chosen to destroy our day? We put undue pressure on our kids to keep us happy (or at least to behave well so we can pretend to be happy). But this expectation is misaligned. The truth is, if we are living by emotions that are based on circumstances, we will inevitably be disappointed.

If we didn't put so much pressure on our children to accomplish what they were never intended to, I think we'd enjoy them a lot more. We'd see that accidentally spilled glass of milk as a quick cleanup job rather than as something to snap a photo of, post on social media, and rant about how all of life with kids is messy. In that moment, we have a choice: we can take the situation in stride, or we can make the dangerous jump to the thought that life isn't what we hoped it would be. Cue depression. Then our kid says something that normally wouldn't be a big deal, but we're already spinning out of control. Cue anger. And then we see our kid's face and realize we messed up. Cue sadness and guilt. And finally, cue wanting to throw in the towel.

In these moments, we need to hold on to the truth of Romans 8:6: "The mind set on the flesh is death, but the mind set on the Spirit is life and peace" (NASB). We will never find life or peace if our minds are consumed with every fleeting emotion that vies for space there.

Maybe you've already tried this whole setting your mind on the Spirit thing and it just didn't take. Elisabeth Elliot emphasizes why it's hard to capture thoughts: "The taking of captives is not a gentle business. They don't want to come."[2] In other words, we have to expect a fight as we change our thought patterns. We need to show up dressed for battle, not with our yoga pants around our ankles.

Here are two specific ways we can be proactive about allowing the Lord to change our thoughts.

1. We need to make room to really contemplate.

Even when we attempt to bring our minds to truth, we often cut things short before truth takes root. When we start sensing that our emotions are taking over, we might throw up a surface prayer like "God, please help me! I'm so frustrated!" I can't tell you how many times I've done this, and when I got to "amen," I felt nothing. Now, this isn't a bad prayer. God hears our cries—even the ones tossed up in quick desperation. But we also need to set aside intentional time to give our brains space to think. For me, thinking is a lost art. I love to read, to consume, to produce. But as I've begun to take time to process what I'm learning, it has activated more change in me than simply reading all the materials I thought would bring transformation. I know this might sound impossible in your noisy home, but in some ways it requires less energy than many other things we try in an attempt to find freedom.

So the next time you find yourself hiding in the bathroom trying to regroup, remember that because of the power God has given you, you are capable of resisting the downward spiral. You don't have to sulk in a Grumpy Mom happy hour; you can acknowledge the emotion without letting it determine your response. This might mean taking a second to think about why something stirred up so much anger in you. In this way, our emotions can alert us to an issue instead of dictating our actions. When we do this, our emotions actually serve us instead of the other way around.

2. We need to acknowledge that deeply ingrained thought patterns will take time to change.

Habits are formed when we repeat something over and over again. We learn this principle when we want to develop a good habit, but it works in reverse, too. It will take some time to remove our negative thought patterns, since they were likely formed over a long period of time. So take heart—even if the progress is slow, it doesn't mean you aren't being transformed. It may just take longer to rewrite your thought patterns than you expected. When you fall back into old habits, don't buy into the lie that you'll never change. Remember that this is all part of the process.

Sure, we'll all get upset again at some point. But let's say goodbye to the hour-long (or day-long!) visits from Grumpy Mom. Let's choose a steadfast spirit that is overflowing with truth so that life's hiccups don't knock us off kilter. It's possible to have victory over our thoughts, but only if we set our minds on the one who never changes.

ACTION STEPS

1. **Recognize patterns.** Are there certain places, times of day, or circumstances that tend to trip you up? Recognize them and suit up for them. I love this version of Psalm 27:3: "When besieged, I'm calm as a baby. When all hell breaks loose, I'm collected and cool" (MSG). Let's tuck this away and bring it to mind during the craziest parts of our days.

2. **Create a list of grounding affirmations.** Don't worry, there isn't anything woo-woo about this. I'm just talking about starting the day with Scripture to lay a firm foundation. Write down a verse and put it on the bathroom mirror, or put it on your phone. You might even voice-record it so you can listen as you get dressed in the morning. Even if you don't have time for a deep dive into Scripture, fill your morning tank with a few solid truths that will set your feet on a steady path.

3. **Excavate the emotions.** Remember, emotions aren't bad; they are purposeful and beautiful. The idea is not to become a robot who doesn't feel things. So how do we experience emotions without letting them destroy our lives? The next time emotions well up that seem set on controlling you, ask yourself a few questions:

    - What is the emotion?
    - What does that emotion want you to do? If you let the emotion dictate your behavior, what would it have you do?
    - What is the truth you need to base your actions on?

KEY VERSE

The mind set on the flesh is death, but the mind set on the Spirit is life and peace.

ROMANS 8:6, NASB

PRAYER

Father, you created emotions. Just like any other good thing you have designed, they can be harmful if I allow them to be my master. Please make me aware of how I let my emotions rule me, and give me a steady heart that is calibrated to you. In Jesus' name, amen.

Chapter 2

THE INCONVENIENCE
OF KIDS

Say Hello to Flexibility

CAN WE TALK FOR A MOMENT about the flexibility the last month has required in our house? After weeks of on-and-off sickness, Christmas vacation arrived. I mustered every ounce of energy I had for two weeks with the girls cooped up at home. The weeks prior had zapped the twinkle in my eyes and the carols from my lips. The girls had perfectly timed their illnesses so that one was always full of combustible energy while the other wanted to be held all day. That meant I was forever trying to balance playing with a healthy, energetic girl and snuggling a sick one. I moved too fast for one and too slow for the other. And then, to make the juggling act more complicated, another ball was thrown in: it was the busiest work month of the year for me.

So when Vana woke up sick the day before returning to school, I lost it and dropped all the balls. I lost it again when her big sister, Vivi, got sick the moment Vana was better. And again when the following Monday was a holiday. And again when we got *snow* of all things in South Louisiana—and with it, multiple snow days.

We were homebound for one solid month. And we're not talking about the summer, when there are camps and activities and pool time and the ability to be outside for ten minutes. We're not talking about a planned break where I cut back on work since I knew the kids would be home. We're talking a month of unscheduled, sick-infested winter days in the middle of a busy work season.

I could talk your ear off for thirty minutes about the tragedy this has been. In fact, I've been talking to a lot of people about it. I'm pretty sure all of them are thinking the same thing: *Get. Over. It.*

Correction. All my friends except Ashley. Ashley is my tough-love gal. Her saying is "I can bring the balloons to your pity party, but that won't help you out." So now you get the idea—she shoots straight. After hearing me whine for the umpteenth time about my bleak winter, she sent me a GIF of balloons. "Consider this the balloons to that pity party! I don't even have anything to say to encourage you, because I would totally be making sides and buying chips if I'd had the days you have been having."

We laughed about the GIF, and then in true Ashley fashion— one of the reasons I love her so much—she said, "Just shake it off—it's mind over matter. And for lack of a better term, suck it up and get it together! I mean, there isn't anything to do about it, and if you sit in it, the devil is winning. So literally just say out loud, 'Nope.'"

Nope, things don't have to be perfect for us to find joy. Nope, we don't need to complain for days on end. Nope, we don't have to wait for our unwanted circumstances to leave for Grumpy Mom to leave.

I'm coming to this realization super late, in true Valerie fashion, but it looks like I have at least one more snow day to learn this lesson. Or maybe more? Who knows what's coming next week! (I say this with a hint of cynicism, but I hope you find it charmingly flexible.) Today I wrote on my calendar "Day of Fun." It's a reminder to me that this day isn't ruined just because it didn't turn out the way I had planned. It's a reminder that doing something I didn't have in mind can still be fun. This feels rebellious and even reckless for a planner like me, but that just shows how deep my need for control goes. Touché, world. You had me fooled, but today . . . nope.

DIVINE INTERRUPTIONS

I don't know what your nemesis is when it comes to flexibility, but for me it is hands down my kids' naps (or at times, the lack thereof). This is the intersection where I have struggled so much with wanting to stick to my own plan. My work hours are relegated to (or should I say dictated by) nap time. I could have an important e-mail that really can't wait, but when Vana wakes up, I know I have precious minutes before it's time to get her. This feels unjust. People need me to respond. I'm not sitting on the couch eating popcorn. *I'm doing Kingdom work, people!*

And then Proverbs 19:21 catches my attention: "You can make many plans, but the LORD's purpose will prevail." If what we planned doesn't happen, then it wasn't God's purpose for that time. Our frustration comes because we feel we should be doing something different from what we're doing in the moment. We struggle because what we think we're supposed to be doing has been interrupted.

But can we grab hold of the reality in this verse? If my plan gets interrupted, then it wasn't *his* plan for that moment after all.

I'm a dreamer. I have big goals, and more times than not, my kids get in the way of those plans. There have been wake-up calls that interrupted my quiet times. There have been perfectly cued tears that came just when the food arrived at the restaurant. There have been fights that broke out the moment I had some pithy idea for an Instagram post. These scenarios felt very much like inconveniences to my beloved life. I can get so focused on reaching my destination no matter the cost that I miss the idea that my purpose—or rather, the Lord's purpose—is to be right there responding to and loving on my kids.

We know this. I think we really do. But we have about a thousand chances a day to forget it.

When Vana was a month old and I had to jump back into work, I read *Treasuring Christ When Your Hands Are Full* by Gloria Furman. As I read, her words hit me: my kids are not an inconvenience. I would like to think this was obvious. I mean, of course my kids aren't an inconvenience! But as I started looking back over my days, I realized I had, in fact, been viewing my kids as an inconvenience. Or at the very least, I sure reacted as if I believed that were the case.

I was working so hard trying to get everything to fall in line with my plans that there was no possible chance I could enjoy my life and the gifts God had given me. So really, it wasn't the inconvenience that kept me frustrated; it was my insistence that everything work out according to my plan.

When we surrender our own plans to God's ultimate (and much wiser!) plan, we are basically telling him that we trust him. This is not small potatoes, ladies. Those moments we see as complete inconveniences are actually opportunities to glorify God.

I don't believe God created us to set our plans in place and follow every single one to the letter, leaving a string of casualties in our wake. If we were able to pull off everything we set our minds to, we wouldn't need him so much, would we? We could put the coordinates in our GPS, bid God adieu, and keep trucking along toward our destination, since we know exactly where we are headed anyway.

Here's my question for you, in tough-love Ashley fashion: Has this method worked for you in the past? Has it worked for you to be in control? Or did you make excuses when things inevitably fell apart, saying it was the kids who made everything chaotic? Did you find some scapegoat to blame? If your life is anything like mine, I'd venture to guess that the perfect circumstances have never come. And I'm pretty sure things won't go as planned in the future, either.

Here's the hard truth I'm coming to grips with: I am needy. I wake up each day not knowing if nap time will be thirty minutes or two hours. It's life on the edge, I tell ya. And because of that, I'm constantly dependent on the Lord. If I tried to do motherhood on my own, I'd be angry 90 percent of the time. I'd be trying to create alternate routes and emergency plans and spending priceless energy making new plans when things go awry. In reality, however, the unpredictability of children is something we should be grateful for, because it reminds us how much we need the one who really is in control. And this is right where we need to be.

In our weakness, he is strong. Isn't this the anthem of every Christian facing a challenge? I think it specifically applies to the way we seek to control our plans for the day, the month, and the year. In my inability to perfectly map out my life, I see that God is strong. Our weakness is calling us to lean on God, moment by moment. The seasons when I have felt the most inept and incapable have been the times when God showed up in big ways.

I learned about flexibility the hard way just after Vana's birth. Just four days after her arrival, we found out Tyler's dad had cancer. When she was six weeks old, we found out the cancer was terminal. And four weeks later, he was gone. It was the heaviest season of our lives. I spent hours bouncing a brand-new baby and praying for her grandpa to be healed. Practically speaking (not to mention emotionally), this season required a lot of flexibility at a time when I thought I needed routines and to have my husband come home consistently at 5:30.

Under normal circumstances, I have no trouble making my needs known. I can convince myself that what I'm up against is the biggest priority and that other people should get on board too. But in that moment, there was no debate. If there was ever a time when selfish Valerie knew better than to put her own needs ahead of others, this was it. My needing a little break from a baby could not compare to the sorrow around me. Even before Tyler asked, I knew that whatever we needed to do in that season, we would do it. That didn't mean I suddenly became super-momma, but it did mean I had to become helplessly surrendered to the Lord. As I did, I felt him carry our family through that difficult time in a way that was far greater than anything my own plans could have accomplished.

TRAVELING WITH TWO MILLION

Let's talk about those Israelite moms who walked through the desert for forty years. With kids. Can you even imagine? The dust alone overwhelms me. And that's to say nothing of the makeshift homes. You have to be the definition of flexible to be a part of a traveling group of two million people.

When I try to put myself in the Bible stories I've heard for thirty years, I quickly realize that what I take as normal (i.e., me making a plan and then following it to the letter) is not normal, at least according to biblical standards. I hate to say it, but we're a bit entitled, friends. Our culture would lead us to believe that having things our way is completely normal and that not having things our way is a reason to pitch a fit. It's countercultural to think that we should surrender our plans to the Lord.

Flexibility may not be a fruit of the Spirit, but it is a character trait that oozes Jesus. It involves being selfless and loving. It reminds us that life doesn't revolve around us. It helps us put the needs of others first. It also reveals a life that is surrendered to God's plans. It's a way of saying that we understand God's ways are higher than our ways, that we don't, in fact, think we're smarter than God.

This idea of surrender is something we need to remember all throughout the day—as we long for control over when we wake up, when we work out, or even when we can go to the bathroom. As we surrender our will and our control to God, he gets the glory. Good can still come even when it's not the good we planned. (I say *can* here, not because I doubt whether God is capable of doing it, but because if we are clawing our way back to our own plans, we will likely miss it.)

We are serving our kids not just for their benefit but because we love the Lord and we know that as we do so, we can glorify God.

ABOUT TO LOSE MY DIGNITY

Do you ever feel like all the shots are being called by tiny dictators in your life—by people who demand snacks and rides and help finding their missing shoe? I feel like this on a daily basis. Not only is it exhausting to respond to their every whim, but their demands violate my very dignity. I feel justified in overthrowing my two little dictators who are making the orders even as they can't wipe their own behinds. After all, God put me in charge of these kids, right? I'm not their employee to boss around. *I'm* the boss.

But then Paul goes poking holes in my mind-set. Philippians 2:7 says that Jesus stripped himself of all privileges and rightful dignity. He loved us so much that he gave up the status he deserved for a bunch of sinners. Including me. His dignity was rightful—in other words, he'd earned it; he deserved it. But he gave it all up because of love.

Being a bit more flexible doesn't mean being a doormat; it takes great strength to serve and to choose to be Christlike. Am I willing to forsake my so-called dignity when I'm called to do so? Can I take two seconds before reacting to evaluate whether God is asking me to give up my dignity in a particular situation? Is this a time I need to stand firm for my kids' souls, or is my relentlessness simply a response out of my own pride?

Decide now that you will strive for flexibility. Pray for it. This may not come naturally for you, but the alternative— stubbornly keeping a grip on your plan—will be your greatest liability. It will cost you your joy, your humility, and your peace of mind.

However, if you can be flexible when things don't go your way (just on the off chance they won't), you open yourself up to a world of possibilities. Being flexible may add extra laughs to your life, extra memories to your memory bank, and extra energy to your relationships. When we view our interruptions from this perspective, every inconvenience gives us an opportunity to look a little more like Christ.

ACTION STEPS

1. **Make yes your default.** I don't know about you, but my
   instinct when my kids ask for something is to say no. Most
   of the time this isn't because there's anything wrong with
   their request; I simply don't want to be inconvenienced.
   For the next week or so, start saying yes to your kids
   whenever you can. You will quickly see that not every
   battle is an important one. When you consciously stretch
   that muscle of losing your dignity, you will become more
   prepared for the times when you're forced to be flexible.
   You'll bend, but you won't break!

2. **Try to set yourself up for success.** One thing I've been
   learning is that if I try to do precious work when I know
   I'll be interrupted by my kids, it will only lead to frustration for all of us. Flexibility doesn't mean you have to learn
   to do the work with your kids at your feet while wearing
   a fake grin and saying, "No, no. It's fine. I can write a deep
   theological post while you ask me about which Disney
   Princess is my favorite based on their dress color." I've
   tried to write blog posts with a toddler on the floor, and
   it boxes us in every time. I need her to be quiet, and if
   she isn't, I feel inconvenienced. Maybe flexibility means
   being flexible about when the post gets written or if it gets
   written. When I change my expectations about what I can
   realistically do, I am able to savor both the set-aside work
   time and the time with my kids. I'm able to enjoy my kids
   more without feeling like they're interrupting anything.

3. **Each morning, ask God, "Okay, what's the plan for
   today?"** When we ask the Lord about his plans for the day

instead of saying, "Here's the plan, Stan!" it allows us to approach the whole day with a much more flexible mind-set. As we surrender to his plans, we're reminded of his sovereignty and prompted to be flexible, knowing we're not the most knowledgeable being in the conversation.

KEY VERSE

You can make many plans, but the LORD's purpose will prevail.

PROVERBS 19:21

PRAYER

Father, wash away my pride and my desire to keep my dignity and my to-do list intact. Teach me how to be flexible. Thank you in advance for working in me and for the joy this new flexibility will bring to my life. In Jesus' name, amen.

Chapter 3

GIVE ME ALL
THE MASSAGES

Say Hello to True Comfort

I NEVER FULLY APPRECIATED hour-long massages until I had kids. I thought they were too long and, honestly, kind of boring. Blasphemy, right? Now that my world is quite a bit more chaotic, I have a few favorite comforts that I treasure up like gold—a massage being one of them, along with a hot Epsom salt bath in the evening, a good book, and my favorite blanket.

When I get the comforts I feel I'm due, all is right in my little world. When these comforts are threatened, however, I spike up like a porcupine and try my hardest to protect what I feel I deserve. But as I read the Gospels, something strikes me: Jesus didn't talk much about comforts. In fact, some of his most faithful followers lacked not only a nice Swedish massage but were actually beaten and thrown in prison instead. (I'm looking at you, apostle Paul). I can hardly imagine what Paul would think if he time-traveled to today! Would he consider us lukewarm in our faith, the way John saw the Laodiceans (see Revelation 3:18-22)? Would he wonder what all the fussing and complaining is about without a prison cell in sight? Would he think it audacious that we expect life on earth to be a walk in the park? Would he think we've gotten so cozy here that we've completely missed our mission?

This is me, more often than I care to admit.

My expectations for motherhood are completely counter to God's approach. When it comes down to it, many of my greatest frustrations are birthed out of the idea that I should be comfortable.

In order to find freedom from Grumpy Mom, I need to release my grip on my comforts and instead cling to the truth. This isn't going to be easy, because I love my comforts. Or, more accurately, many times I *live for* these comforts. The things that separate me from God aren't usually "big" sins. More often it's my love of comforts and the comfortable life.

Here's what this looks like for me: I look at a cabinet of groceries but consider the shelves all but bare because there isn't a lime LaCroix to soothe me. I sulk because I have to drive my husband's tin can of a car. I prioritize a relaxing night to myself over serving a friend who really needs me. When these things happen, my love of comfort takes a dangerous turn from enjoying refreshing gifts from God to being something I spend my life searching for.

The world constantly tells us that contentment will be within our reach once we feel comfortable again. Once we attain that desired level of comfort, we should freeze everything and hunker down. When we face seasons of feeling unsettled—waiting for a job, waiting for a baby, waiting for a home to sell, waiting for a doctor's report to come back—we should just try to get past those uncomfortable moments until we can get back to our comfort zone again. We can't fathom that these hard parts of the journey are actually part of the bigger plan.

Paul puts it this way: we are adamant to get back to "civilian affairs." And yes, we're going to hear more from Paul, because the guy sure knew a thing or two about suffering. Here are the instructions he gave to his mentee Timothy: "Join with me in suffering, like a good soldier of Christ Jesus. No one serving as a soldier gets entangled in civilian affairs, but rather tries to please his commanding officer" (2 Timothy 2:3-4, NIV).

I don't usually consider my life a battleground, and the parts that do feel like a battleground seem more like interruptions to my comfortable life. For example, on days when it's a thousand degrees outside and I'm trying to cram a cart full of groceries, a toddler who has never been buckled in without screaming, and a big sister who has her own agenda (which doesn't include sitting down) into the car, I get angry because my comfortable life has been disrupted. When my deepest longing is for comfort, it's hard not to spew onto everyone in my path.

The problem isn't the inevitable moments of discomfort; it's that I am not prepared for them. I have to stop believing that trials are the exception to the rule, when really they're just part of life.

The greatest irony of all this is that comfort is found in God. He doesn't promise that life itself will be comfortable—just that he himself, through the Holy Spirit, will be our comfort. In 2 Corinthians 1:3-5 Paul says, "Blessed be the God and Father of our Lord Jesus Christ, the Father of mercies and God of all comfort, who comforts us in all our affliction, so that we may be able to comfort those who are in any affliction, with the comfort with which we ourselves are comforted by God. For as we share abundantly in Christ's sufferings, so through Christ we share abundantly in comfort too" (ESV). I hope this truth brings freedom instead of disappointment. Yes, we will face affliction in this world. But God promises to bring us comfort in the midst of whatever we're going through. That means we can stop fighting for every moment to be comfortable and instead accept the comfort God promises.

I'm filing this away for the next time an uncomfortable moment of motherhood makes me want to turn into Grumpy Mom. Maybe it's the burden of too many potty breaks for your newly trained kid, a nursing baby who wants to be fed at the most inconvenient moment, hot weather that drains every bit of your energy (can you tell this is a big one for me?), the constant eye rolls from a teenager who thinks they know better, or the extra pounds around your waist.

God gives us strength to respond with grace.

He gives us the power to experience joy and gratitude, even in the hard moments.

THE SUNDAY STRUGGLE IS REAL

I came across a well-intentioned post on Facebook the other day calling moms of littles to give themselves grace if they don't make it to church much when their kids are young. The post went on to say that it's the other six days that matter more for how our kids understand Jesus. It was meant to make me feel better, but ironically it made me uncomfortable. It seemed to support the idea that church is optional based on our level of comfort and ease. I'm not advocating for legalism here, but this mind-set almost makes way for hedonism and doing only what feels good.

In a world of political correctness and wanting to make sure we don't step on toes or make moms feel bad, we've gone soft on truth and hard on grace. I should clarify here that yes, I am a huge proponent of grace. It's only by grace that we can accept the gift of eternity—and abundant life on earth, too. But I'm afraid we use grace cheaply sometimes in an attempt to make everyone feel more comfortable, when in reality our comfort isn't at the center of God's plan for our lives.

Perhaps one of the reasons we tend to make an idol of our comfort is because we feel like we are entitled to it. John Ortberg puts it this way: "The bigger the sense of entitlement, the smaller the sense of gratitude."[1] This is certainly true for me. I don't typically thank God for a supportive bra, toast for breakfast, or even my next breath. I thank him for big opportunities I never thought I'd have. The rest of the gifts I've been given I see as run-of-the-mill things I deserve.

This view affects how I respond when comforts are taken away from me too. I can't possibly respond well when I lose something that I felt like I rightfully earned or deserved. If I think I deserve clean floors, then tiny crumbs on the floor will be a source of great discouragement. If I think I deserve a two-year-old who knows the rules, then one who naturally rebels will undo me. If I think I deserve an uninterrupted quiet time each morning, then any distraction will leave me feeling let down.

The best way to release our expectation for a comfortable life is to realize we don't deserve it and to be grateful for what we do have. A life not focused on our comforts shouldn't scare us; it should remind us how limited our view is and how much better equipped God is to call the shots for us. I want to be excited for the life God has for me—even if it includes blowout diapers, too-loud dinners, and a lack of massages.

This shift in perspective will transform our motherhood. We can't walk through the hard moments of life knowing God is in control without feeling a sense of joy. That's something I'm not entitled to but am super grateful for.

THE PURPOSE OF SUFFERING

If you've been a mom for more than twenty-four hours, I'd venture a guess that you know motherhood brings with it the highest of highs and the lowest of lows. The fact that we love our children so much also means that they can cause us the most anguish. Whether you're dealing with a defiant toddler or a prodigal teenager, at some point you will face suffering as you parent your children. When you feel weary from those relentless, hard moments, I want you to be encouraged and remember the good that can come from suffering so you will keep fighting for it.

Philippians 1:29-30 says, "It has been granted to you on behalf of Christ not only to believe in him, but also to suffer for him, since you are going through the same struggle you saw I had, and now hear that I still have" (NIV). As we look at the full context of Philippians 1, we see three benefits that come from enduring trials:

1. **Suffering yields proven character.** When we suffer trials, we will get to see how the Lord is growing our character. When this happens, it motivates us for the future as we realize what we've already overcome.
2. **Suffering isn't a punishment but is something granted to us.** While suffering may feel painful, it is purposeful and intentional—a tool God uses for our benefit. In the same way that we won't let our children eat only junk food, God sometimes gives us things that help us grow, even if it's not what we would choose.

The good fruit always outweighs the hard things we're experiencing.

3. **Suffering reflects Jesus' life.** When we're in the midst of suffering, it may be tempting to think that God doesn't understand or is blind to our pain. But any amount of suffering we experience pales in comparison to what Jesus endured on our behalf. Our suffering can remind us of the Cross and cause gratitude to spring up in our hearts.

TENTS WILL BLOW OVER

When I read Mark 13 recently, it challenged me to think about my comforts. This passage is about the end times, and it gives an illustration of a man who goes on a journey and leaves the servants in charge, commanding them to stay awake, ready for his return. Verse 33 says, "Be on guard, keep awake. For you do not know when the time will come" (ESV). I was intrigued by what exactly it means to "keep awake." I mean, yes, I get that we are to live with an awareness of eternity. But what does that look like in everyday life?

Here's what Matthew Henry's commentary says: "Our great care must be, that, whenever our Lord comes, he do not *find us sleeping*, secure in ourselves, off our guard, indulging ourselves in ease and sloth, mindless of our work and duty, and thoughtless of our Lord's coming; *ready* to say, He will not come, and *unready* to meet him."[2] I shuddered a little as I thought about how my comfortable life is such a focal point for me. If it's too cold, I grab a sweater. If it's too hot, I crank up the AC. If my kids are yelling, I try to get us back to Comfort Level 10 as soon as possible. I'm not recommending a ban on indoor climate control, but it's concerning that on many days, my comfort is my singular mission.

I think what's going to set us back as we strive to live in expectant hope of eternity is feeling so comfortable on earth that we forget this is only temporary. We'll end up spending our time finding just the right curtains for our tents instead of inviting everyone we know to the housewarming party of all housewarming parties in heaven. Loving our lives is not a bad thing, but the depth of love will be directly proportional to the depth of devastation when the stream of comforts shuts off. And the degree to which we depend on earthly comforts will be proportional to the amount of grumpiness we feel when we lose them.

Will we be shocked when the wind knocks over the walls of our tent? Will we let it send us spiraling into a pool of tears, or will we keep a heavenly perspective and remember that this is only a tent?

The reality is, we can't be obsessed with God's purposes and our own comforts at the same time. One will inevitably take priority. But when we turn our eyes heavenward and remember to "keep awake," we suddenly become warriors and our comfort level is no longer our top priority.

THE GRASSHOPPER COMPLEX

Before you get the idea that we should all long for a life of suffering, we also need to be careful not to swing in the opposite direction. Sometimes we assume that if we aren't suffering as moms, we aren't doing it right. We assume that motherhood will be miserable from start to finish, so we refuse to allow joy or gratitude into our hearts.

I've had some seasons in my life when God showered my

family and me with really good things, but I couldn't let myself enjoy them. I was sure things should be harder, so I just gritted my teeth and waited for the other shoe to drop. As ridiculous as this may sound, I don't think I'm alone in this. At dinner with a group of friends recently, one friend unloaded that it felt hard to pray for financial provision. Her family has real needs, but knowing that they are better off than people in many other countries, she felt uncomfortable praying for more. We all shared how we've held back with God ourselves because we felt like we didn't deserve some of the blessings we've been given. I told her about my inevitable thought spiral when things are going unusually well in the Woerner house: I assume I'll die or contract some life-threatening disease any moment, because surely so much goodness couldn't happen to me.

Have you been there? This idea isn't biblical, mommas.

So we have to manage the tension of believing that life should be a gravy train of comforts and believing that if we aren't suffering enough, we're doing it wrong. In either case, we aren't clinging to God. Either we're clinging to our comforts, or we're clinging to our suffering.

We can take the pressure off our comforts in either direction by placing our hope solely in Christ. When we acknowledge that God is the origin of all the good things in our lives, it allows us to enjoy life's little pleasures that much more. We can even find joy in the hard moments because we're able to see that God is bigger than our suffering.

The pastor at our church once shared about what he called the grasshopper complex. The book of Numbers describes twelve spies who went to check out the land of Canaan that God was giving to the Israelites. Joshua and Caleb came back, saying, "Let's go at once to take the land. . . . We can certainly conquer it!" (Numbers 13:30). The other men? Having seen the same thing, they decided trouble was ahead: "The land we traveled through and explored will devour anyone who goes to live there. All the people we saw were huge. We even saw giants there, the descendants of Anak. Next to them we felt like grasshoppers, and that's what they thought, too!" (Numbers 13:32-33).

What we focus on determines our outlook. Have you heard the tale about the two salesmen who went to another country to see if there were any opportunities to sell shoes there? The first man quickly wrote a letter home, saying, "No one here wears shoes. There's no one to sell to. I'm coming home." The other man said, "No one here wears shoes. There's a huge market! Send shoes!" We have a choice: we can see the challenges we face as opportunities or as obstacles.

I want to view both the suffering and the comforts that come my way through the lens of God and his purposes. I don't want to be overly focused on the suffering or the comforts, because when I make either too big, I find more reasons to try to escape this motherhood life and hide out in my closet. Instead, I want to live with my eyes on Jesus—unafraid of losing my comforts and seeing the opportunity that can come from suffering.

ACTION STEPS

1. Think through these questions:

   · What demands do your kids make on you that trigger your anger and make you feel like their servant?
   · What comforts would you struggle to live without?
   · Is there anything uncomfortable you have been putting off doing? What's one step you can take toward accomplishing that goal?

2. **Do one small thing that takes you out of your comfort zone today.** A life of comforts has a way of making us fearful of everything. Decide to do without one of your daily comforts (e.g., coffee, chocolate, Netflix, social media) and replace it with something that will have more lasting value. Keep challenging your comforts so you don't end up dependent on them.

KEY VERSE

I have told you these things, so that in me you may have peace. In this world you will have trouble. But take heart! I have overcome the world.

JOHN 16:33, NIV

PRAYER

Father, give me eyes to see that my life is about more than just my comforts. Give me a heart that desires more than my comfortable bubble and instead longs for the Kingdom work you have for me here on earth. In Jesus' name, amen.

Chapter 4

HANDS ON LIKE A HELICOPTER

Say Hello to Worry-Free Parenting

WHAT IS IT ABOUT MOTHERHOOD that instantly catapults us into new realms of worry? Sure, I used to worry before I had kids, but now I can ratchet up to a ten in no time flat when there's a threat that involves my girls. And if there's one thing that especially rattles my nerves and causes the blood to rush to my head, it's anything related to their health.

Not long ago, we noticed some irregularities in Vivi's heartbeat, so we took her to get tested. Now, this would have been enough to put me over the edge anyway, but my cousin had recently passed away in her twenties from an unknown heart condition. I just wanted answers. I wanted a clear-cut explanation that would put my fears at rest. I wanted some doctor who was way smarter than I am to discredit me as paranoid so I could put my sweet girl to bed without incessantly putting my ear to her chest to make sure her heart was working correctly.

After the test, the doctor let us know that it would take a little time to get results and that we shouldn't panic if we didn't hear anything for a while. Taking a while is a good sign, he said. If it was serious, they'd contact us immediately.

Less than twelve hours later, I got a call from the nurse. Instantly my insides sank and my limbs grew numb. Isn't it crazy the way our fear manifests itself in such physical ways? I picked up the phone, expecting the worst. Was the diagnosis fatal? Was this a chronic condition that would leave me wondering if I'd lose her at any time? In a matter of seconds, I flashed to how life would change once we got the bad news. I had almost mentally packed my bags for a long stay at the hospital, and it felt like my own heart was ready to burst out of my chest. So I did the only thing I could in that moment. I took a deep breath and stepped into the unknown, holding the Lord's hand. I surrendered this to him, because it was just too big for me.

"Her condition is absolutely harmless," the nurse informed me while I held my breath.

I could hardly believe what I was hearing. It was the best scenario we could have asked for. There really was an arrhythmia there—I wasn't a crazy mom for noticing it. But it wasn't harmful.

We had a happy ending to that story, but it pointed out to me how quickly fear can take over any sense of reason. Maybe you've had a scary call or situation too, and maybe your most dreaded nightmare came true. The truth is that an underlying sense of worry can consume us, whether it's about small things or big things. The world tells us that we moms have no choice but to be overbearing worriers about even the most insignificant of things.

I don't know about you, but it's often the little things that keep me in a constant state of unrest and distraction, and eventually result in overwhelming negativity. Will that fever turn out to be a sign of something fatal? Is that bump on her head not getting bruise-y because it's swelling on the inside, in her brain? Is her belly sticking out not because she had a full meal but because she has the same condition as the little boy I heard about who lost his life last year? I've had all these thoughts and could rattle off a dozen more, but I'm afraid you might close your book for an impromptu physical exam of your kids by Dr. Mom Shaking-Hands, MD.

If we have any hope of experiencing true joy in motherhood and living differently from the world, we need to renew our thinking. For starters, it might help to know it's actually possible to be a mom who isn't always filled with worry for her kids.

Do you know who I wouldn't consider helicopter parents? Mary and Joseph.

Here's a story about their parenting style for the Son of God:

Every year Jesus' parents went to Jerusalem for the Passover festival. When Jesus was twelve years old, they attended the festival as usual. After the celebration was over, they started home to Nazareth, but Jesus stayed behind in Jerusalem. His parents didn't miss him at first, because they assumed he was among the other travelers. But when he didn't show up that evening, they started looking for him among their relatives and friends.

When they couldn't find him, they went back to Jerusalem to search for him there. Three days later they finally discovered him in the Temple, sitting among the religious teachers, listening to them and asking questions. All who heard him were amazed at his understanding and his answers.

His parents didn't know what to think. "Son," his mother said to him, "why have you done this to us? Your father and I have been frantic, searching for you everywhere."

"But why did you need to search?" he asked. "Didn't you know that I must be in my Father's house?" But they didn't understand what he meant.

Then he returned to Nazareth with them and was obedient to them. And his mother stored all these things in her heart.

Jesus grew in wisdom and in stature and in favor with God and all the people.

LUKE 2:41-52

Can you even imagine the headlines if this scenario had happened today? Mary and Joseph traveled an entire day's journey without realizing their son had stayed back in the town they were leaving. They no doubt would have been labeled terrible parents (or worse!) on social media. Who knows—maybe some people would have even called for Jesus to be removed from their home. And it definitely would have been the hot gossip of the local church.

Something that really catches my attention in this passage is that good can still come even if mom is scared. Our comfort level is not a reason to keep our kids from living and growing.

Mary and Joseph felt frantic over Jesus' disappearance, but the teachers he talked with in the Temple were astonished by him. I wonder what those people who heard Jesus did next. I imagine they shared their experience with others or let it change their lives in some way. Had Mary been like me, she would have known where her son was the whole time. This might have prevented her from being worried (until something else came up, of course), but she would have deprived Jesus of the opportunity to impact the people in the Temple.

Here's something else I notice in this passage: Mary benefited from this situation too. She was able to experience even more gratitude for Jesus (once she calmed down a little). The passage goes on to say that when they were back in Nazareth, Mary "treasured all these things in her heart" (Luke 2:51, NIV). Maybe after this trip to Jerusalem, she appreciated her son more. Maybe she soaked up the minutes with him.

Despite all the parental nerves, there was so much good that came out of this situation. As I am learning to be less afraid, I can take a cue from Mary's experience in letting go. My mind might take a little longer to catch up, but it's possible to not let my fear determine the decisions I make for my kids.

CAREGIVING OR CARETAKING?

So what is actually happening when I perpetually tell my kids no in an effort to keep my own fears at bay? Maybe sometimes it's not even a big fear, just the desire for calmness. Vivi constantly asks me if she can crack the eggs when we cook, and I've refused for so long because this inevitably causes a mess—and there's a chance we'll get salmonella. When I do this, I'm essentially prioritizing my own desire for a calm, stress-free existence over my kids' opportunity to develop into mature adults. Now don't get me wrong. This doesn't mean that if our kids want to jump off the roof we're supposed to say, "Go for it. I won't let my pesky old fear stand in your way!" We just need to be aware of the undercurrent of fear and ask ourselves this question as we make decisions: Is our priority a calm situation or our child's growth?

Although I like to think of myself as a fairly laid-back mom (Tyler, stop laughing!), this question gets me. How many times do I say no simply because I don't want another thing to worry about? Nancy Groom calls this the difference between caregiving and caretaking. Caregiving is doing for others what "they cannot or need not do for themselves," while caretaking "operates on the assumption that his or her way is the only way." She goes on to say, "Caretakers insist on preventing other people's mistakes."[1] Now that I know the difference between these two ideas, I'm recognizing how easy it is to be a caretaker instead of a caregiver.

When we claim responsibility for something, all other parties involved take notice and subconsciously back off. The master of the task has been determined, so everyone else can tune out a bit and just wait for orders. That's why I can't get to my mother-in-law's house without a GPS despite having ridden there shotgun with Tyler countless times. Because if I'm not driving, I check out. That's the reason Vivi acts as if she can't dress herself even though she's perfectly capable. Out of my own fear of getting to school late, I insisted on doing it for her for too long. Our fear can handicap not only us but anyone standing in our path. We can't have it both ways. We can't be caretakers when it's convenient for us (in other words, when it calms our fears) and then wish our kids would fend for themselves when it's appropriate (i.e., when we have no fears). As I take inventory of my parenting, I'm noticing just how many beasts I've tamed that I now have to house, feed, care for, train, heal, and pay for.

Can I tell you about the peanut butter beast? Vivi and I eat apples and peanut butter every day. For the past year, I've dipped her apple in the peanut butter for her (even though she can do it herself), because heaven forbid she get too much peanut butter or smear it all over her knuckles, which we all know will end up on the whitest piece of fabric in the room. Instead of simply teaching her how to do it, I've been the peanut butter rationer. I've stopped my own snack midbite to get her a slice. I've walked across rooms. I've put down her baby sister. I've dropped everything I was doing. All to make sure her peanut-butter-to-apple ratio was precise and not indulgent or messy. I realize this is a silly example, but it is tuning me in to how many other similar beasts I've tamed and how they keep me from finding margin in motherhood.

As my kids get older, I know my control will gradually lessen. I want to foster in them an ability to make decisions and live a life of following God. Giving them more choices and responsibility will help them learn to do that. We can find untold freedom when we start relinquishing control instead of having it ripped from our white knuckles.

These are the benefits of not giving in to our fears, but perhaps the biggest one is that we can discover a life untethered. I like the sound of that. And who knows—maybe I'll have less peanut butter on my own yoga pants as I stop rationing the goods.

GOD'S IN CONTROL; I'M NOT

Have you ever noticed there's a bad kind of feeling small (when we hear about all the terrible things going on in the world) and a good kind of feeling small (like when we realize we aren't God but we know the one who is)?

I love Psalm 121. It always makes me feel small in the best way as I see how big God is. It opens with these words: "I lift up my eyes to the mountains—where does my help come from? My help comes from the LORD, the Maker of heaven and earth" (NIV).

As we look at the mountains or the ocean or even the clouds in the sky and the grass beneath our feet, knowing that God made it all, that perspective can swallow up any fear we have.

The closing words of this psalm are just as meaningful to a mom like me who struggles with wanting to control all the variables: "He will watch over your life; the LORD will watch over your coming and going both now and forevermore" (Psalm 121:7-8, NIV). Not only is God big enough to create the heavens and the earth, but he's personal enough to care for us and our kids. God's attention captures the big-picture things ("your life") and the everyday things ("your coming and going"). There is literally not a moment when the Lord's eyes aren't on us. This brings us peace because we know that the only things that happen are the things that God allows to happen.

Still, in the fearful moments of life, I tend to forget that God is in control. I might know this truth in my head, but that's not enough. I have to really believe it's true.

Just like Jairus did.

Mark 5:35-43 tells the story of a man with a very sick daughter who went to find Jesus so he could heal her. While he was with Jesus, messengers from his house came to tell him that his daughter was dead and that he no longer needed to bother Jesus. What strikes me about this story is that even as his daughter neared death, Jairus ran *to* Jesus. Isn't that a great metaphor for us, too? This poses a question for me: Do I turn toward God or away from him when things get hard?

When Jesus overheard this news, he told Jairus, "Don't be afraid. Just have faith." Peace came *before* healing, as Jesus instructed Jairus to go home. This prompts more questions for me: When do I have peace? In the midst of the trial or only after I get the healing or the answer to prayer? And if it's after, isn't there always something more to worry about?

When we know Jesus is with us, peace can come even before we know if everything is fine. If you are struggling with anxiety right now, consider this your training ground to learn to live at peace before you get the go-ahead from your circumstances. You have the go-ahead from God—it's written all over his Word. The Bible tells us more than three hundred times to not be afraid. We don't have to live in fear because (a) God loves us and (b) he's in control.

GOD IS A BETTER MOM THAN I AM

Let's get uncomfortable for a moment here. I know I'm not the only mom who thinks about death. The idea that something could happen to me freaks me out more than anything else. Not for my own sake, because, hi, I'll be in heaven. I know I'm headed to greener pastures. The reason death scares me so much is because I can't imagine how my kids would survive without me. Yes, I know they'd live. Tyler is a great dad. But pride has me consumed with the thought that without me, their lives would be a shell of what they should be. I don't admit this in casual conversation, but it's something that often hovers in my subconscious thoughts.

And when I dig a little deeper, here's what my morbid thoughts reveal: control is a pride issue. It stems from the idea that I am the best person to handle all the pieces of my life. The more we get to know God, the more we understand his power and love, and the more we recognize the depth of sin he has rescued us from. It's only then that we are able to come humbly to him, knowing we can't make it on our own. When we shed our pride, we can relinquish control, because we know God will do a much better job than we could ever do. This truth isn't just meant to comfort us if the unthinkable were to happen. It can mark a shift in the way we parent right this very minute.

Here's the reality: God is a better mom than I will ever be. I realize that is a politically incorrect thing to say, but you get the idea. He is able to love my kids better, discipline them better, comfort them better, and counsel them better than I ever could. I want to hover a little less, knowing that God has the best view—and the best rescue plan, if needed. He has appointed me to be a steward of these kids, but at the end of the day, they are ultimately his.

PRAYER, DUH

I heard somewhere that 85 percent of the things we worry about never happen. Goodness, that means I've been wasting a lot of emotional energy on things that never even come to pass! There's a short phrase in Max Lucado's book *Anxious for Nothing* that has altered my thinking when it comes to anxiety: "Fear sees a threat. Anxiety imagines one."[2]

As I've felt overwhelmed by different situations lately, I have tried to put this idea to this test. Is this a genuine fear that I need to respond to, or is it something I'm imagining? Am I spending countless moments lost in worst-case scenarios that most likely won't happen? Am I letting that anxiety steal away my kids' mom when they need me most?

The good news is that anxiety doesn't have to have the final word in our hearts and minds. Here is the anthem of every worrier:

> Do not be anxious about anything, but in everything
> by prayer and supplication with thanksgiving let your
> requests be made known to God. And the peace of

God, which surpasses all understanding, will guard
your hearts and your minds in Christ Jesus. Finally,
brothers, whatever is true, whatever is honorable,
whatever is just, whatever is pure, whatever is lovely,
whatever is commendable, if there is any excellence,
if there is anything worthy of praise, think about
these things.

PHILIPPIANS 4:6-8, ESV

With the help of the Holy Spirit, we have the ability to protect
our minds. This is hard to actually choose, but the process is
actually pretty simple. First, we need to know that it is possible
to live in peace. Then we can look at what we're allowing in our
minds that is causing us to doubt God's goodness and eliminate
it. After we cut out the bad stuff, we need to fill up our minds
with the good stuff—the truths in God's Word. Finally, we need
to pray. Every time we feel the tug of worry on our hearts, we
can use that as a trigger to bring our concerns before the Lord.

The difference between prayer and worry can feel pretty
small at first glance. Both involve thinking about the same thing,
but when we look at what's worrying us in the presence of the
Lord, it suddenly feels much smaller. When I take a worry and
turn it into prayer, I'm passing it off to God. It's no longer my
problem. In reality, it was never mine to take on in the first place.

As we seek to be moms who are defined by peace rather
than anxiety, we need to remember that this isn't a "try
harder" kind of scenario. The transformation comes from the
work God is doing inside us. Isaiah 26:3 says, "You will keep
in perfect and constant peace the one whose mind is steadfast
[that is, committed and focused on You—in both inclination
and character], because he trusts and takes refuge in You [with
hope and confident expectation]" (AMP). Perfect and constant

peace? This doesn't sound close to my default setting. Even when I do all the things—reading the right verses and praying like crazy—I can still be completely consumed with the thing I fear. Apparently I am a good multitasker.

If that sounds like you, take heart—God can fill you with a peace you have never known. Commit to setting your mind on him, no sideshows, and watch what he will do.

And y'all, by now you should know that this isn't a one-and-done thing. We have to keep choosing peace over and over again. Every time our kid climbs too high on the ladder. Every time our kid faces a bully at school. Every time our kid hops in the car with a friend.

But whatever the circumstances, we can keep choosing to live in the peace that the world may never experience—a peace that God gives us even in a world of unknowns.

ACTION STEPS

1. **Pray for your kids.** When we lift up our kids to the Lord, we can rest in the knowledge that he loves them and is protecting them. You might want to record your prayers for your children in a prayer journal to mark the ways God has been faithful. (See page 254 for resources.)

2. **Remove the badge of honor from worry.** Stop imagining worst-case scenarios in the name of protecting your family. Instead, pray that the Lord would fill you with his peace and that if there is real danger, he will alert you to it.

3. **Let a free spirit lead.** If you tend to be more cautious as a parent, make sure your child has time with someone who is more of a free spirit—whether that's their

dad or a relative or a family friend—so they can spread their wings. I'd suggest letting them do this without you there, because (in my case at least) momma might interfere. Sometimes that momma-bear instinct can't easily be tamed.

KEY VERSE

You will keep in perfect and constant peace the one whose mind is steadfast [that is, committed and focused on You—in both inclination and character], because he trusts and takes refuge in You [with hope and confident expectation].

ISAIAH 26:3, AMP

PRAYER

Lord, I long to be a mom who isn't constantly worried about my kids. I am starting to recognize that my fears come when I take wrongful ownership of gifts you've given me to be stewarded. Give me the faith of Hannah, who dedicated her beloved son Samuel to the Lord. My kids are yours. It's hard for me to fathom this, but you love them even more than I do. That means I can put my full trust in you, knowing you will take better care of them than I could through all my worrying. Bring peace to my mind, and remind me that worrying only steals precious undistracted moments I could have with my kids. I put my trust in you. In Jesus' name, amen.

PART TWO

REPLENISH

Chapter 5

YOU DON'T HAVE
TO BE JOAN OF ARC

Say Hello to True Self-Care

TAKE A MOMENT WITH ME to think back on the baby showers you've been to. It seems like inevitably, when seasoned moms get together, the floodgates open. After a while, the mom-to-be is sitting there thinking she officially made the worst decision of her life—one she can't take back. Okay, most people don't actually put it so bluntly, but with all the discussions about sleep (or the lack thereof), the way a baby will affect your marriage and work, and the prospect that you'll never go to the bathroom alone again, you start wondering why the human race continues at all.

Most of the time these conversations are tied up with a bow that this is all worth it. As if you just watched a horror movie and the victim, who has been running around fearful and tortured the entire time, ends the film by saying, "This wasn't so bad! There really were some good parts." (To be fair, I have no idea if that's what happens in horror films, because technically I haven't seen one in fifteen years. But I can't imagine that any of them actually end that way.)

We don't have to look far to encounter the myth that motherhood is synonymous with martyrdom. We take the biblical idea of serving our children and laying down our lives for others to an unhealthy extreme and assume that we shouldn't spend time taking care of ourselves (until the kids go to college, maybe).

In most cases this idea comes from a good heart, but it can easily get blown out of proportion. We want to be appreciated. We want people to know how hard we work for them, so we make sure to remind them at every turn. We compete with other moms to see who will win—and by win, I mean the mom who has it the hardest.

I've heard all of these phrases in the competition for Martyr Mom of the Year:

- "Be glad you have girls. Boys are so much harder."
- "Oh, you are so lucky your kids are sleeping."
- "It must be so easy working from home."
- "Having three is like a thousand times harder than having two." (This one may be an exaggeration, but it has definitely been said with the eyes!)

Plenty of times I've taken these comments as invitations to fight for the coveted title. The thing is, though, no one wins when we try to compete over who has it hardest. Perhaps you made a very convincing case that your motherhood tragedy ruled the day. Congrats. Or maybe you listened to the most depressing story of motherhood ever, only to find yourself racking your brain, trying to tally up the reasons why your life is in fact harder than your opponent's. Either way, everyone loses.

We have to stop competing.

If our goal is to find approval from other people, we will never end up victorious. Your husband or your mom or your best friend may never understand how hard you work. And even if they do, those pats on the back will still leave us wanting.

We cannot do motherhood for the praise.

No earthly praise will ever feel like enough for all we do as moms. So rest, friend. Stop fighting for it. If we don't, we will turn into negative-focused, attention-starved women who dwell on the hard moments and file them away so we can bring them up later when someone forgets how hard we work.

I speak from experience here—I've done this, and it never makes me feel better.

WHY WE FALL ON THE ALTAR OF MOTHERHOOD

It's easy to associate self-care with selfishness. (It's practically in the name, after all.) Because of that, it can be a struggle to untie the two. One realization helped me as I was wrestling through this. In *Emotionally Healthy Spirituality*, Peter Scazzero says that Jesus disappointed people. This rubbed me wrong at first, but when I looked at the Word, I realized it was true. Luke 5:16 says, "Jesus often withdrew to the wilderness for prayer." Not just once, but often. Even the word *withdrew* sounds prickly and kind of selfish. I'm sure Jesus could have healed more people and impacted more lives if he hadn't withdrawn. But would he have had the power, the might, the energy, and the focus to do all that without readjusting his eyes heavenward?

If Jesus himself needed refreshment, doesn't it make sense that we, too, need to steward our bodies, minds, and souls (the biggest resources God has given us)?

The tough truth is, we can make the things we really care about happen. Case in point: if I want to get up early to watch the royal wedding, I will forgo prior commitments (like sleep) to make sure it happens. So this leads me to believe that sometimes we simply don't want to make self-care happen. I know what you're thinking: *What mom wouldn't want to take care of herself?* But *wanting* self-care isn't the issue. The issue is what we have to sacrifice to make it happen. And most of the time it's not the usual suspects like time or money that get in the way. More often, it's pride.

This brings me back to a Saturday morning when I was early in the process of writing this book. The content was still relatively fresh on my heart, but the devil was at work trying to discredit everything I wanted to share. I had been feeling overwhelmed by too many tantrums, too many nos, too many middle-of-the-night wake-ups. I had been super snappy with my kids and my husband. Everything was a burden. I felt like a victim. I was tired and just wanted a few minutes of quiet.

The only thing I could think of to reset my attitude was to hand the baton to my husband and leave for an hour or two. I didn't need a vacation from my family; I just needed a break from the grumpy mom I was becoming. But as soon as I voiced to Tyler my need for a break, the negative voices in my head set in.

I wrestled with guilt for needing to step away for a while, especially since I'm preaching that you don't have to escape to a desert island to find peace.

I felt weak for not being able to stay in the tension and just put on a happy face.

I felt embarrassed, knowing my husband could probably handle this better than I could.

As I headed out the door, trying to fend off these accusations, I realized something: these are the thoughts that trap us. This is why we don't take care of ourselves—because we feel like we should be able to handle the pressure on our own.

If you're a single parent, if your husband works long hours, if you're new in town, or if you live far from family and it's difficult for you to get away, maybe you assume you should be able to manage the stresses of motherhood without a break. The world feeds us the lie that we should be self-sufficient and able to manage everything on our own. This might seem heroic, but it reeks of faithlessness and pride. The truth is, God designed us for community. We are intended to serve others and to allow them to serve us, too.

That doesn't mean it's going to be easy. Some situations will require more creativity than others, but trust the Lord to handle this. He wants you to be dependent on him, and in doing so, he will likely use human beings to deliver that tangible help to you. Your role is to strip away your pride and accept help as the gift it is.

Can I admit another reason why I refuse to take care of myself sometimes? I like having credits in my account.

This past week my husband and I were both really busy. Usually we are in a pretty good flow, where we take turns being busy. I knew it was going to be a stressful week for Tyler, so I told him to go ahead and work late, leave early in the morning, and just take care of business. As the week wore on, I desperately needed some time to work myself, but I insisted I could make the sacrifices. Did I do this because I'm such a selfless person? One look at my passive-aggressive responses to my husband would tell you that this was not, in fact, why I did it.

So what was going on here? Leverage. I needed an edge— something I could bring out at a moment's notice if needed. Maybe I'm the only one who likes the company of leverage, but ultimately this kind of manipulation doesn't bring about the freedom we are looking for. The only way to transform ourselves and our families is to be honest and admit when we need help.

And maybe there's just one more reason I try to do it all on my own: because I'm scared of looking too relaxed or too put together. We expect every mom to stick with the status quo. We are all exhausted. We are all wearing yoga pants with no makeup. We all have dry shampoo–saturated hair. We are all sitting in our minivans in the carpool line, sipping cold but much-needed coffee. We are all grumpy. I'm scared that if I don't stay in line, someone will judge me and look too closely at my life to see the reason. I'm scared they will assume I'm forgetting something big. I'm scared of being judged—period. Being different is scary.

Here is the question we have to answer: Do we care more about what others think of us or about becoming who God created us to be? Sometimes I wonder if we sacrifice the opportunity to live more abundantly because we don't want people to judge us or assume we have it easy. Let's accept the lifelines we've been given and thank God for meeting our needs, one day at a time.

THE 5 P.M. FETAL POSITION

How is it that Tyler can be gone for two days on a fishing trip and I can have the kids in bed early and be cool as a cucumber . . . but if he gets home from work forty-five minutes later than I expected, I suddenly can't handle life and I hand him a baby as soon as he walks in the door? Subconsciously, I think I see my husband's lateness as disrespecting me or not appreciating that the delay means more work for me. Whatever the reason, it comes from a heart that desperately longs to be appreciated and will do whatever it takes to remind people why I deserve such appreciation.

Right after that flood I mentioned in chapter 1, Tyler talked to me about wanting to help a pastor friend whose church and community had been completely leveled by the storm. I wanted him to help too, but as we talked about it, he didn't really acknowledge the sacrifice it would be for me if he were gone another Saturday after a summer of missed Saturdays. That's when the show started—the one where I overexaggerate how hard I work and how much I do. In times like these, I feel like I have to stomp my feet to be heard. It's true, I had been working my tail off, but when you're trying to prove something, all gestures get bigger. Your child's five-minute tantrum morphs into a thirty-minute meltdown as you recount the story.

Our job as moms can be thankless and taken for granted. So we talk about how little sleep we get and wear it like a badge of honor. We harp about spit-up-stained shirts and dirty hair and lack of makeup. I have done this too many times to count. But then out of nowhere, God will prick my heart, and I'll feel overwhelmed with gratitude that he would entrust these little souls to me. And then I'll feel another prick and remember that Tyler isn't out having a skip day or lying on a beach reading a good book. He's dealing with demands of his own—and probably a few tantrums from bigger humans. Another prick reminds me that I actually have fun with my kids, and not getting to do the work I'd planned to do just means I'm doing something else that is good.

Every prick to my heart plants joy back into my soul and makes me feel a bit ridiculous that I fight to see all the hard stuff instead of the good stuff right in front of me.

ALL OR NOTHING?

Here's the thing. Neglecting yourself is not a badge of honor. We shouldn't revel in skipping meals or never having time to finish a book. Realize right now that even before you change what you do, you can change the way you talk about it. God has called us to be mothers, not martyrs, and we have more say about self-care than we think.

While I was pregnant with my second child, a hot bath was my favorite way to get comfortable. I'd take two or three a day. I had a two-year-old at the time, and I'd simply say, "Grab your crayons, Vivi. Momma wants to go take a bath." And she'd grab her crayons and coloring book and park herself in the bathroom next to me. Inevitably she'd start chatting or dropping crayons in my bath. It wasn't quite the peaceful, candlelit bath some people dream of, but it worked. I took care of myself, and she learned to be flexible too.

I can think of other times when I have failed miserably at taking care of myself, and usually what it comes down to is that if it doesn't look the way I pictured it, I choose not to do it at all. This is where we run into many of the struggles of motherhood. We can't leave our kids for the entire day, so we don't take even an hour or two to go out with friends in the evening. We can't go back to school to get that degree we've been dreaming of, so we don't even consider the online class we can fit into our fringe hours.

There is a tension to manage when it comes to self-care, because we don't want to swing to either extreme. On the one hand, we can fail to take care of ourselves in a healthy way, and on the other hand, we can selfishly demand our way all the time. After a week of having both girls home—fussy girls, at that—I can find myself being overindulgent when it comes to time alone. It's simply not realistic for me to have hours alone to myself every day at this stage, but taking an hour is possible.

On that evening when I told Tyler I needed to leave for a while, I went to the coffee shop to read and journal. I was gone about an hour, and when I walked back in the door, I was a different mom from the one who had left. I wasn't gone long, but it was long enough for my spirit to shift. My tank was refilled, and I was ready to pour into others again. That time was worth it—for my husband, my kids, and me.

Don't feel ashamed of your weakness or the times you need to get away to reset. After all, those places of weakness are where God meets us. I love this paraphrase of the Beatitudes: "You're blessed when you're at the end of your rope. With less of you there is more of God and his rule" (Matthew 5:3, MSG). The passage goes on to say, "You're blessed when you get your inside world—your mind and heart—put right. Then you can see God in the outside world" (verse 8, MSG). See that? God blesses us when we tend to our minds and hearts. In other words, when we put our inside world right, we are able to see God's view of motherhood, not simply the world's definition. That's hardly selfish or indulgent.

If you struggle to feel worthy of quality time for yourself, tuck these verses somewhere close and be willing to get creative to find that time. It won't be easy, but it's worth it. *You're* worth it.

ACTION STEPS

1. **Do something that really refreshes, not pseudo-refreshes, your soul.** Hello, smartphone. I am rarely refreshed by screens in general. I've started asking myself, *What's the one thing I can do now that, if it's the only thing I do with my free time, will refresh me for the remainder of the day?* This has led me to use ten minutes of my ninety-minute nap breaks to read instead of just

working or doing chores. Stealing ten minutes out of my work time is hardly noticeable when I look at my home or my e-mail, but it makes all the difference for my soul.

2. **Don't be afraid to let your kids see you working, and incorporate them into that work.** Life isn't one big board game, and you are not the game master. In other words, our role isn't to entertain our kids and create a twenty-four-hour Disney-like experience for them. I have to remind myself that it's not just okay for my kids to see me working (and to work alongside me); it also builds character. Reject any lie that says you're being selfish when the mundane things of life happen in front of your kids.

3. **Stop believing the lie that our kids are the reason we don't take care of ourselves.** Saying, "These kids have kept me so busy it's been days since I've had time to wash my hair!" is the mom-conversation-starter equivalent to "How about this weather?" I was never put together or dressed to a T before I had kids, but now I seem to think my kids are the only reason I'm not pulled together. It's an easy out. The next time you're tempted to make an excuse to this effect, own it and reflect on your unique personality. For example, you might say, "You didn't know me then, but in college I was quite the tomboy. All I wore were torn jeans and white tank tops, and I'm pretty sure I didn't own a dress." This might seem out of left field, but it redirects the conversation off a negative view of our kids. Our joy will be restored if we stop seeing ourselves as victims and stop seeing our kids as a hindrance to our self-care.

KEY VERSE

You're blessed when you get your inside world—your mind and heart—put right. Then you can see God in the outside world.

MATTHEW 5:8, MSG

PRAYER

Lord, I am yours! Help me to see myself the way you see me and value myself the way you value me. I have confused being unselfish with misusing the very body and mind you gave me to steward well. Thank you for reminding me that I am worthy of being cared for. Now, Lord, I need you to show me how to do this. In Jesus' name, amen.

Chapter 6

WHEN THEY CRY,
I EAT CHOCOLATE

Say Hello to Real Satisfaction

WHEN IT COMES TO WHERE we find satisfaction, most moms could be divided into four camps: (1) those who rely on coffee, (2) those who rely on chocolate, (3) those who rely on wine, and (4) those who *have* to be lying, because it's definitely one of those three.

I fall in line with the moms who find sweet relief in chocolate—specifically, in a fancy chocolate bar from Whole Foods and a lime LaCroix. It's my nap time cocktail and signals "me time."

Now, there's nothing wrong with chocolate (God came up with the idea of the cocoa bean, after all). The problem comes when I start treating my chocolate fix as something I need in order to be happy. I believe the lie that something God created instead of God himself will be my saving grace when I'm stressed or overwhelmed. But I am always disappointed by my little idol, because the satisfaction lasts only a moment. Then I'm left trying to fend off Grumpy Mom with only an empty dark-chocolate-with-toffee-and-sea-salt wrapper. This never goes well.

DE-CHOCX

In the fall I did a ten-week reset with a nutrition coach. This meant, among other things, no chocolate for two and a half months. Goodbye, sweet relief.

Those first few days were pure torture. We've already talked about what an emotional train wreck I can be under ordinary circumstances. You should have seen me detoxing from chocolate. Part of me was angry at myself when I realized how much I "needed" something that wasn't God. How had I become so dependent on something so inconsequential? How could my whole day be wrecked as a result of not having this thing that isn't mentioned once in the holy Word of God?

After a few days, though, I started seeing some progress. As I ate my spinach salads with homemade dressing, chia seeds, and veggies, I was no longer throwing toddler-style tantrums or cursing. I was getting more even tempered, and it felt good.

But there was a catch—I found a substitute. Nothing saccharine, but it was still extra refined. *Frasier.* Yep. That old '90s show about the lovable but snooty psychiatrist. I couldn't eat my simple salad without it. I traded one satisfying treat for another.

Again I was reminded of my need for satisfaction. What's embarrassing is that I have a whole chapter in my book *The Finishing School* about chocolate and my lack of self-control. I learned a lot about my vice of choice then, but during a rough season after my second daughter was born, it slowly crept back in until I found myself in need of a detox.

Then again, that's the whole point of this book. We aren't going to suddenly have everything figured out. That's why we need daily doses of God's truth—so that when we want to respond like Grumpy Mom, we have the tools we need to change the way we react, to rewrite the script.

That desire for something to satisfy us isn't going to go away, but we need something more than chocolate. We need something that will truly satisfy.

Vivi says this phrase that makes her sound much older than her four years. She'll start to tell me something, and then before she finishes, she says, "Yoooou know." As in, "You know what I'm about to say, so I'll wait for you to fill in the blank."

So friends, I'm telling you. *Yoooou know.* Yoooou know what I'm about to say. We have to find satisfaction in God alone. But guess what? That knowledge isn't going to get us anywhere until we discover what that actually means. So let's break it down to the foundation and build up some walls.

WE NEED A FOUNDATION, AND WE NEED WALLS

We need two things to live satisfied in Christ before we reach for the coffee (or wine or chocolate): spiritual grounding and a practical defense.

We need a foundation that plants us firmly in our choices. Luke 6:48-49 says, "It is like a person building a house who digs deep and lays the foundation on solid rock. When the floodwaters rise and break against that house, it stands firm because it is well built. But anyone who hears and doesn't obey is like a person who builds a house right on the ground, without a foundation. When the floods sweep down against that house, it will collapse into a heap of ruins." Without a solid foundation, the house is swept away. It is fine until the littlest bit of weather change. We need to make sure this isn't us. Motherhood is unpredictable, and we won't find joy in it by chance. We have to be intentional about building a firm foundation on God's Word, because if we don't, we'll be swept away by the lies of this world.

Once we have a foundation, we need walls and boundaries that give us a definitive plan of action. Proverbs 25:28 says, "A man without self-control is like a city broken into and left without walls" (ESV). We need a plan that makes us less vulnerable to attacks in the first place. And our plan can't be flimsy. We can't pitch a tent; we need to build solid walls. As moms, we know we'll face moments that make us want to yell and curse. (I use the example of cursing a lot, and I'm afraid I'm going to get quite the potty-mouth reputation!) The way to fight Grumpy Mom is not to escape permanently; it's to redirect our hearts back to God's best on a daily basis— especially when we feel the tug to let our circumstances determine our reactions.

So how are we going to build walls to protect our minds from the lie that coffee (or wine or fill-in-the-blank) is going to get us through a rough day? Let's start in Galatians, where all good talks on freedom start. Galatians 5:16-18 (NIV) says, "Walk by the Spirit, and you will not gratify the desires of the flesh. For the flesh desires what is contrary to the Spirit, and the Spirit what is contrary to the flesh. They are in conflict with each other, so that you are not to do whatever you want. But if you are led by the Spirit, you are not under the law." As believers, we are not under the law. Therefore, our flesh is at a disadvantage. Let's relish and rest in this fact!

My detox is over now, and chocolate is back in my life. I still enjoy warm cookies and the occasional episode of *Frasier*. The difference though? I treat these things more like gifts from a mighty God than as gods themselves. When they ultimately point me back to God instead of stealing my attention away from him, the very things that used to enslave me have become avenues of worship. What if we got crazy and really celebrated the wonderful things God has given us, like bubble baths, fresh-out-of-the-oven cookies, pedicures, and sweet tea, without thinking these things will be our saving grace? What if we could remember that all this is a sweet gift from the one who offers us the saving grace in the first place? What if we could enjoy the little things God gives us without the post-guilt realization that we've warped something good in a way God never intended?

We can find freedom when we realize it's possible to enjoy God's gifts without making them crutches as we face an exhausting day with the kids. With this newfound freedom, we'll be able to savor the gifts instead of cramming them down our throats like a forget-me pill, like we're trying to wash away our sorrows. It's possible to enjoy our blessings when we don't depend on them for the satisfaction of our souls.

So what does this look like, practically speaking? Here are two protective walls I've built to help me handle my chocolate crutch:

1. **I don't indulge when I'm grumpy.** That is pretty cut and dry—a good wall to put up that might help you, too. If I eat chocolate when I'm grumpy, I do so hoping it will fulfill what only God can fill. And once I'm done, I'm not left feeling grateful for a treat; I'm left feeling empty because it didn't do what I'd hoped it would. And what about those times I spend all morning joyfully pining for the moment when nap time will start and I can crack open an ice-cold LaCroix and

unwrap pure joy covered in foil? I'm not grumpy, but I'm still looking for some satisfaction in an afternoon treat. That's when it's time to consider #2.

2. **I pray about my relationship with chocolate.** This might sound a bit over the top and maybe like something those rule-loving Pharisees would come up with, but prayer is the quickest way for me to align my will with God's. It's in prayer that I am finally able to surrender something I've been fighting tooth and nail. Sometimes when I'm done praying, I'm able to dive straight into a sweet treat, filled with gratitude to the Lord for the little blessings in my day. My bit of nap-time chocolate is satisfying, but only because I enjoyed it in the Lord's presence. But maybe on other days, I realize as I'm praying that I'm looking to the chocolate to satisfy me, so I decide not to partake in that moment. God gets the glory when we make tough decisions like that. (And we're still just talking about chocolate!)

The freedom we can find here is life changing, mommas. In a world that's happy with surviving (cold coffee in hand), we can thrive and enjoy every good and perfect gift from the Lord. Mom life is deep. It is countercultural. And above all, it is truly and abundantly joyful.

STUCK IN QUICKSAND

Will you indulge me in one more conversation about our favorite crutches? Let's get dramatic for a minute. If coffee (or your vice of choice) and your time with the Lord (let's just say your Bible here, for a visual) were stuck in quicksand, which one would you save? Put another way, which one do you rely on to save *you*?

We all know the right answer here, but in the middle of a chaotic day, I can see myself being tempted to choose chocolate, with the awareness that it provides immediate relief. The Bible, on the other hand, offers long-term fulfillment. I'm not saying we won't ever experience immediate peace or find flashes of clarity when we read the Bible. But the truth is, sometimes the less significant things seem like a more instant win. That's why if we are ever going to gain freedom from the idols in our lives, we need to shift our minds to what satisfies us in the long term.

This is not a modern problem—it's a pattern we see throughout the Bible.

Esau learned the hard way about seeking instant relief. He traded his birthright for a bowl of stew (see Genesis 25).

Daniel faced a similar temptation, but he handled the pressure a bit better. When he was taken captive and forced to eat the king's food, he made a plea to eat the foods of his people instead of food that would defile him according to Jewish law. He requested that if he was healthier and stronger than the other men after ten days, he would be allowed to keep eating his own food.

Here's what happened: "At the end of the ten days, Daniel and his three friends looked healthier and better nourished than the young men who had been eating the food assigned by the king. So after that, the attendant fed them only vegetables instead of the food and wine provided for the others" (Daniel 1:15-16).

Are you as impressed as I am? The man was in a foreign country as a captive. I would have been reaching for all the bread and all the pasta to drown my tears in. I wouldn't have been asking for a salad. But Daniel knew what he really needed—he knew what would satisfy him. He knew what would make him stronger and healthier. And he didn't sway, even with a buffet of options in front of him.

This commitment reveals so much about Daniel's heart to glorify the Lord with every choice. As the rest of the book of Daniel shows, God blessed Daniel with health and nourishment.

There is an application here for us, too. True nourishment is passed on to us through the Lord; it doesn't bypass him. Any substance that bypasses the Lord isn't going to be ultimately satisfying.

THE GOD OF THE BELLY

When I get to heaven, I think I'm going to be like that annoying girl in class who asks all kinds of questions about things that won't be on the test (or, you know, things that won't matter once I'm in the presence of the Almighty but I still want to know out of curiosity). My journalism education taught me to have a question ready pretty much all the time. You should feel a little sorry for my husband.

Anyway, what I read this morning brought up one of those questions. Matthew 4:23-25 says,

> Jesus traveled throughout the region of Galilee, teaching in the synagogues and announcing the Good News about the Kingdom. And he healed every kind of disease and illness. News about him spread as far as Syria, and people soon began bringing to him all who were sick. And whatever their sickness or disease, or if they were demon possessed or epileptic

or paralyzed—he healed them all. Large crowds
followed him wherever he went.

Here's what I wondered: Did the large crowds that followed
Jesus include those he had healed? Or were they perfectly
happy to get healed physically and then go on their merry way?
I mean, no more seizures, the ability to walk, no demons? That
sounds like a pretty nice life. But was it enough for them? Or
did they sense that if Jesus could heal their physical needs,
there was actually a greater prize: the man who did all these
things in the first place? Were they content with the gift, or did
they want to know the giver?

And perhaps more to the point, what about me? Do I try to
find solace in something inanimate, like chocolate, or in the
one who dreamed up the cocoa bean? Again, that might sound
a tad silly, but all of a sudden, I feel quite ridiculous for relying
on chocolate the way I do while completely ignoring the hand
that offers it to me.

Vana does this too. When she gets really upset, if I fuss at
her or tell her no, she immediately says, "NOONIE!" (her name
for her pacifier). I wish y'all could see the way she waddles
down the hall to her room with those chunky thighs. I'm standing right there to comfort her, and instead she hightails it to
grab what she thinks will satisfy her. (We have yet to broach
the conversation of how she's misplacing her satisfaction by
sucking on a plastic god, but I'm thinking we can wait until she
reaches at least the age of two. Maybe by then I'll be able to
lead better by example.)

You might think I'm overspiritualizing a bit when it comes
to our methods of relaxing and our indulgences. I hear ya. But
as I read the Bible in light of our desire for quick-fix satisfaction, I realize just how important this conversation is.

Philippians 3:18-21 fills me with hope (even as it stomps my awkwardly long and crooked toes): "For many, of whom I have often told you and now tell you even with tears, walk as enemies of the cross of Christ. Their end is destruction, their god is their belly, and they glory in their shame, with minds set on earthly things. But our citizenship is in heaven, and from it we await a Savior, the Lord Jesus Christ, who will transform our lowly body to be like his glorious body" (ESV). *The Message* puts it this way: "All they can think of is their appetites."

This belly that craves chocolate as a way of providing solace on a rough day is part of the very same body that is being transformed to be like Christ's glorious body. He has satisfaction in mind for our renewed bodies that would make chocolate taste like sawdust in comparison.

ACTION STEPS

1. **Test your vices.** In his book *The Compound Effect*, Darren Hardy talks about what he calls a "vice fast."[1] Here's how it works: you choose one of your vices (it could be carbs or chocolate or Instagram or something else), and abstain for thirty days. If it's a real struggle, you may have found something that has more control over you than you think. If that's the case, find someone to be accountable to, bring it to the Lord in prayer, and put some hard boundaries in place until you find freedom.

2. **Acknowledge the giver before the gift.** When you enjoy those little blessings from the Lord, take a moment to

recognize who gave the gift in the first place. This can naturally redirect your heart to the one who can bring true satisfaction.

3. **Meditate on Proverbs 25:28.** What does it look like to be defenseless before your enemies? What would it look like to be a city with intact walls?

KEY VERSE

Our citizenship is in heaven, and from it we await a Savior, the Lord Jesus Christ, who will transform our lowly body to be like his glorious body.

PHILIPPIANS 3:20-21, ESV

PRAYER

Lord, you are the only one who satisfies me! Help me to stop looking to your creation and instead look to you, the Creator, for all my satisfaction. When I feel empty and start seeking fulfillment, help me to focus on you. Reveal to me the things that I have looked to for refreshment, and give me a passion to come to you—the one who gives generously and waters my weary soul. In Jesus' name, amen.

Chapter 7

ON EMPTY

Say Hello to More Energy

GROWING UP, I was terrified of becoming a mom. Not because of how kids change your life, challenge your confidence, and require loads of knowledge and attention. Nope. Those realizations came later. What terrified me was the no-sleep thing. I liked my sleep. When I was a kid, I dreaded slumber parties because I knew I'd have to pretend to be having so much fun that I had no desire to sleep, when in reality my sleeping bag sounded much more fun than a Matchbox Twenty dance party. In college, I never pulled an all-nighter. In my opinion, no grade was worth losing my beloved sleep.

So when I got pregnant, I spent months pleading with the Lord for a good sleeper. When I was twenty weeks along, I remember two separate conversations with friends who gave me their thoughts on energy and rest when it comes to motherhood. One of them said, "You fall into bed every night utterly exhausted," and the other said, "You just kind of get used to the lack of sleep."

The second friend's comment shocked me. How could anyone be so casual about not sleeping? My friend seemed unfazed by this thing I'd feared for so long. But to my surprise, when I became a mom, I started to experience something similar. Don't get me wrong—I was still tired. In fact, when Vivi was a few weeks old, I had to unfollow someone on social media who kept posting about being tired and how little her kid slept. In my fragile state, I knew I'd pounce on any opportunity to join the choir of moms lamenting about their tiredness. Instead, I tried to focus on my friend who had somehow adjusted to the lack of sleep. Her words kept ringing in my ears, and she became a beacon of hope for me.

I soon realized that there's a lot more to finding energy than getting sleep. Yes, it's important for us to get rest. And yes, we should sleep as much as we can for a thousand reasons. But my guess is that your newborn doesn't care much about the science behind REM cycles, and your sick kids don't schedule their wake-ups at convenient times. But rest easy, tired mommas with the early risers and the midnight partiers: energy isn't just found in connecting with your pillow. You can beat the idea that all mommas are tired and that tired mommas can't function.

I remember experiencing my first breakthrough in this area when I was dancing in the kitchen while making breakfast with my kids. This wasn't normal for me. I was usually tired and a bit slow at this time of day. But that morning I felt like I had energy to spare—like my bones couldn't keep still even when sleep was in short supply.

Our energy levels determine a lot about what our days will look like. For me, it's a direct decider of whether I take my kids to the park or plop them in front of the TV. It determines whether I see their playful energy as fun or draining. It determines whether I am engaged or distracted.

I'm over not enjoying my kids simply because I don't have the energy for it. Are you with me, momma?

WHAT'S BEYOND OUR CONTROL

What would you say zaps your strength? Is it the kids you can't control? Is it the demands of your work? The soccer schedule? The unending housework? Is it something else you have no power over? I'm getting tense just thinking about all those things. How can we possibly hope to increase our energy if the things that burn us out are things we have no control over? What a discouraging thought!

All those things can certainly play a factor in depleting us, but I can't tell you the amount of energy I've wasted trying to fix things I have absolutely no control over. This cycle exhausts me more. What's empowering is focusing on the things that are within my power to change.

So let's just cover our ears, hum a tune, and ignore all those things we can't change, at least for the moment. I mean, if we can't control them, why give them too much attention? That will drive us bonkers. For now, we're just going to take responsibility for the things we *can* change and that will increase our energy and give us a greater ability to resist those Grumpy Mom moments.

WHAT WE CAN CONTROL

If you're talking to other tired moms, chances are you'll hear them point to external circumstances as the primary reason they're exhausted. But the truth is, there are a lot of internal conditions that exhaust us. These can be more difficult to identify, but the good news is that we have some measure of control over them. In other words, we might not be able to change the soccer schedule, but we can change our attitude about driving our kids to practice every night. If we can identify these soul-level energy zappers, we will be able to start rooting them out.

Harboring Sins

When we harbor unconfessed sin, we create a distance between God and us. Psalm 32:3-4 says, "When I kept silent, my bones wasted away through my groaning all day long. For day and night your hand was heavy on me; my strength was sapped as in the heat of summer" (NIV). This dramatic wording makes me realize that unconfessed sins can debilitate us in a physical way. You've heard me drone on about Louisiana summers, so you know I get it when the psalmist talks about his strength being sapped in the summer heat. This passage is speaking my language. When I am harboring sin, it manifests in me as a hollowness in my chest. It's like the most hungry feeling I've ever known. My energy is gone. But when I feel that God is near, I stand taller and am more capable than I am on my own.

Disobedience

Disobedience is like unconfessed sin, but it's marked by the ongoing sinful choices we make. Elisabeth Elliot says, "Much sickness—physical, mental and emotional—surely must come from disobedience. When the soul is confronted with an alternative of right or wrong and chooses to blur the distinction, making excuses for its bewilderment and frustration, it is exposed to infection."[1] Infections require rest in order to heal. I can't help but wonder how much of my energy is used to stave off spiritual infections brought on by my disobedience.

Fear

Fear is paralyzing. It wraps itself around our brains and keeps us from moving forward. We become consumed by something we can't control, and that fear keeps us distracted from the things we can control. We can't move forward in the present if we are consumed by the future. My pastor, Dennis Malcolm, said recently, "Worry does not remove the stresses and burdens of tomorrow. Worry guts today of your energy and strength."

I felt this in a big way before I conquered one of my biggest fears: flying. For weeks before I was going to fly for the first time in eighteen years, the what-ifs stole every bit of my headspace. I would have been content to lie in my bed and let my fears loop until my flight, but I had a family to take care of, work to do, and a life to live. I had no idea how I was going to make it through this. But God showed up in the midst of my fears, helping me surrender my thoughts to him and giving me a peace I can't explain. With that peace came freedom for me to think about more than just what-ifs. As I released that fear, I was surprised by what a resurgence of energy I felt.

Negativity

There are two types of negativity that will drain your energy: negativity in your own thoughts and negativity from people around you. We talked in chapter 1 about how we need to change our thought patterns. The only way I know of to get rid of internal negativity is to surrender our thought life to the Lord on a day-to-day (and even minute-by-minute!) basis. When it comes to other people, we may not even realize what a big effect they can have on us. Have you ever noticed that certain people immediately bring a smile to your face, while others make your shoulders droop? Which women in your life fuel you and give you perspective? Start recognizing the patterns and intentionally surround yourself with uplifting people.

An Unclear Destination

Do you know where you're going? Do you have a sense for what plans God has designed for your life? If not, it's hard to bother getting out of bed. Of course, making dinner, rocking a baby, picking up toys, and helping with homework day in and day out can feel draining and maybe even a little pointless. But when we recognize God's purpose for our lives, whether it's a specific goal or our purpose in general as followers of Christ, we start to see these activities as worthy endeavors. Making dinner isn't just a chore; it's a way to nourish our family. Rocking a baby is a way to bring comfort and love. Picking up toys is a way to clear the clutter and create white space in our lives. Helping with schoolwork is a way to instill discipline and responsibility in our kids. When we feel motivated about life, we are propelled forward in a way that can't be thwarted by external exhaustion.

Dissension with Others

Any time my husband and I are fighting, I feel instantly drained and want to curl up in the fetal position. Life seems to stop until we are back on the same page. I move a little slower, and I'm too distracted to really hear my kids. My lethargy affects them too—when I'm like this, they aren't exactly bouncing around, ready to tackle the day either.

Our emotions and our bodies and our souls are closely connected. So it makes sense that when something is gnawing at us relationally, it will impact our energy levels too. The same holds true when it comes to a mom or a sister or a friend. If there is tension, especially in a significant relationship, we can't compartmentalize it; it will eventually seep into our ability to be fully present in our daily reality. When we live at peace with others, however, we will inevitably have more energy to devote to the things and people in need of our attention.

Inflexibility

It takes muscle to cling tightly to something that's out of our control. We end up having a tug-of-war between our plan and God's plan. In most cases, whatever we were hoping would happen still doesn't happen, and now we're exhausted.

I love to read books, and occasionally I've fought tooth and nail to read at an inopportune time. My kids would need my attention, and I'd get interrupted before even finishing a paragraph. This frustrates me much more than simply choosing to put the book away.

But when I choose to be flexible—and when I choose this road with joy—I feel a lightness that can't compare with the death grip I once used to hold on to my plans.

Having a Messiah Complex

Are you simply taking on more than God has called you to do? Are you trying to lead where God is asking you to follow? Are you saying yes to all the good things instead of just the best things? I know there are many days when the list of what I think I must do is vastly longer than what God has planned for me for that day. It shouldn't be any wonder that we find ourselves drained, mentally and physically. It's time for us to stop doing what God never asked us to do and ask him what his priorities are for the day ahead.

Allowing Our Virtual World to Take a Disproportionate Role

I feel funny bringing this up because (hi!) there's a good chance I know you through social media. But here is the reality: we can invest so much in people we don't know in real life that we don't have energy left for the people around us.

I have been guilty of this on plenty of occasions. I know everything @inspiringgirl337 did last week, but I'm too tired to ask my husband how his day was. I'm not saying we should give up on social media altogether, but we need to keep this in check to make sure it's not replacing or diminishing our relationships with in-the-flesh family and friends.

Failing to Discipline

Brace yourself—this one is going to get bumpy. (As if the others were a walk in the park!) Proverbs 29:17 says, "Discipline your son, and he will give you rest; he will give delight to your heart" (esv). There is a certain ease that comes from disciplining our kids. Wait, back up. To be clear, I'm not saying that it's easy but that there's an ease that comes with it. When my husband and I fail to discipline, we inevitably feel exhausted and full of dread about the future. We start dealing with our kids in a reactionary way, and that requires us to always be on guard mentally. When we discipline wisely, however, we do so with the hope that we will see our kids transformed.

SOURCES OF ENERGY

I'm pretty sure all of us want to be free from things that steal our strength. But what habits can we practice to bring more energy to our days, even when our circumstances threaten to drain us?

Prayer

Isaiah 40:31 says, "Those who trust in the LORD will find new strength. They will soar high on wings like eagles. They will run and not grow weary. They will walk and not faint." Trusting in the Lord means hoping in him and believing he will do what he says he'll do. Let's start there. Do I believe God can give me strength? How do I try to live out of my own strength? One of the clearest signs that I'm trying to do things on my own is that I assume I'm too busy to pray. Instead of tapping into God's strength by asking for his help, I attempt to handle everything on my own.

I have to admit that prayer doesn't feel very practical to an efficiency-minded person like me. How can praying help me yawn less and keep my head from drooping? It doesn't make sense, but maybe that's because I've been following the patterns of the world too long. E. M. Bounds says, "Prayer is not the opposite of work; it does not paralyze activity. Rather, prayer itself is the greatest work; it works mightily. . . . It does not lull to sleep, but arouses anew for action."[2] Even though I have definitely fallen asleep while praying, this makes sense to me. There is something that propels my life forward as I pray. Spending time in prayer reminds me that God is at work. In the same way that running a race next to someone pushes us forward, God pushes us forward when we're aware of his presence with us.

Abiding

Ultimately, God is our greatest source of energy. That may not sound like an immediate boost compared to a double shot of espresso, but that doesn't make it any less true. When Christ lives in us, that makes all the difference in the way we view ourselves. Philippians 2:12-15 says, "Be energetic in your life of salvation, reverent and sensitive before God. That energy is God's energy, an energy deep within you, God himself willing and working at what will give him the most pleasure. Do everything readily and cheerfully—no bickering, no second-guessing allowed! Go out into the world uncorrupted, a breath of fresh air in this squalid and polluted society" (MSG). This, y'all! I want to daily walk in this reality. I want to live energetically because God himself is "willing and working" in me.

Lately I've felt overwhelmed by too many projects and commitments. As I think through my to-do list, I have to admit that what's wearing me out are things I added on my own. Sometimes we need to downsize—to say no to bigger and better. There is great relief in knowing we can abide in the vine (see John 15) instead of being out on a limb doing our own thing.

Gratitude

Thankfulness changes us. When we're feeling the weight of life, it lifts our spirits and brings energy to our weary bones to recognize our blessings. So set out to find what's good in your day, knowing that the effort won't be wasted. This is a simple practice, but it will energize you.

Confession

When we sin, we're often tempted to respond in one of two ways: either we try to ignore the sin and stuff it down, or we wallow in it, unable to move forward. Confession is the antidote to both of these extremes, as it allows us to deal with our actions head-on and then receive God's grace. In his self-titled book of the Bible, the prophet Nehemiah challenged the people to have joy even as they dealt with the guilt of their mistakes: "Don't be dejected and sad, for the joy of the LORD is your strength" (Nehemiah 8:10). Let confession free you, and don't sit in the guilt of sin so long that it drains you. Find freedom in the grace God gives.

Silence and Solitude

This one might sound easy, but it's perhaps the hardest one of all for me: stop talking and rest. Exodus 14:14 says, "The Lord will fight for you. And you have only to be silent" (ESV). This is reeeeeally hard for me. I tend to see silence as awkward, both with people and with God, and I'll do anything to fill it up. I think I'm helping, but my sorry attempts to strike up a conversation take away from the intentional things that should actually be filling that space. But on the occasions when I've made space to be quiet with the Lord, I've experienced true refreshment—the kind of soul-level energy that can't be imitated by any amount of sleep.

Life-Giving Words

Have you spoken words of kindness today? Words that lift someone else up? When I say something that may offend another person, I become distracted, wondering if I hurt their feelings and what I can do to make things right. This mental back-and-forth takes up headspace. But when I speak words of life, I'm encouraged, knowing that I'm able to encourage someone else. Proverbs 16:24 says, "Gracious speech is like clover honey—good taste to the soul, quick energy for the body" (MSG). Life-giving words can provide quick energy to both the speaker and the hearer. If you are in need of a pep talk, go to that friend who always cheers you on and find energy in a soul-lifting conversation. And if someone in your life needs a little encouragement, you may be surprised to find that lifting them up gives you a boost too.

A Teachable Spirit

Psalm 139:23-24 says, "Search me, O God, and know my heart; test me and know my anxious thoughts. Point out anything in me that offends you, and lead me along the path of everlasting life." If we want to live with a lightness to our days, this is where it starts. Having a teachable spirit means knowing we're not perfect and therefore we don't need to defend ourselves as such. When we are teachable and willing to learn, our loads become light.

Unity

Romans 12:16 says, "Live in harmony with each other. Don't be too proud to enjoy the company of ordinary people. And don't think you know it all!" God calls us to live at peace with one another. Not only is this a reflection of his character, but it also gives us energy to devote to the true battles. When my husband and I are in sync, we're like two wheels on a bicycle, propelling each other forward. We gain momentum together, and with each rotation we make, I find myself energized.

Acts of Service

I learned the importance of serving others when I was big and pregnant with my second child and consumed with my own needs (pregnancy can definitely do that to you). My sister was getting married soon and needed to pick up her wedding dress, but she had a full-time job and would have had to drive across town in five o'clock traffic. I offered to pick it up for her, because sitting in a car with Vivi singing in the backseat was something I could do. What I realized was how much it pumped me up to serve someone else. It was a perfect example of how God renews us as we serve others.

A TALE OF TWO EXHAUSTEDS

No one wants to feel exhausted; we all want to feel energized. But there is one type of exhausted that is beautiful. I want to be exhausted in the sense of doing everything God has asked me to do. When I get to heaven, I hope I have exhausted the plans God had for my life and gone full speed for his Kingdom.

Is there anything better than giving all we've got for the God of the universe?

Exodus 16:19 refers to the way God fed the Israelites when they were wandering in the desert. Scripture describes the manna God sent down from heaven each day, and it records that Moses told them, "Do not keep any of it until morning."

As I read this passage, I came to this revelation: "I can't help but think this is how God fuels our body by giving us enough energy for each day for us to use up completely. Sometimes our lack is not from giving too much away, but clinging too much or hoarding it. I need to trust that God will provide."[3]

The energy God gives us is for today, so let's use it fully. Let's live boldly for the Lord, not hoarding strength as if God won't provide for the next day. I don't want to miss opportunities because I'm trying to conserve energy for tomorrow. We can trust that if God is leading us, he will also provide what we need.

Now, this is not an excuse for us to max ourselves out but a reminder that the Christian life is not a cakewalk. If we are expecting to never feel tired, I'm not sure I'd call that really living. We will certainly face hardships and different seasons that require a lot from us. But when we stay focused on what God is calling us to do, those feelings of exhaustion can be buoyed by the knowledge that we're doing what we're supposed to be doing.

If you're exhausted in a good way—meaning you're living an abundant life for the Lord—then rejoice in it! See that good kind of exhaustion as a sign that you are loving hard and living well.

When I was a wedding planner, my team and I would spend the entire day on our feet, running in heels. Around midnight or so, when I finally fell into bed after a hot bath, I'd feel this strange sensation coursing through my feet. They would hurt, but it was oddly gratifying—like every step I'd taken that day had been worth it. The ache symbolized a day of serving our clients well.

These days, I experience something similar after a full day of doing what God has called me to do—serving my husband in a unique way, playing hard with my kids, meeting a deadline, or pushing myself through the afternoon wall and making it to bedtime with a smile on my face. By the time I go into my girls' rooms at night and stare at their faces in the dim light, thanking God for them, my body might be dead tired. But I'm energized because I feel like I did what God had called me to do that day. The exhaustion is a footnote to how full my soul feels.

Are you ready to get rid of the world's version of the exhausted, grumpy mom and replace it with a healthy kind of tired? As we work to refuel ourselves and find energy, we can also embrace the beautiful breathlessness of chasing after God.

ACTION STEPS

1. **Know your breaking point.** All of us have different levels of what we can handle at each life stage. But we all have one thing in common: none of us can do it all. We need to figure out how much is too much—preferably *before* we get to a breaking point. For example, too many evening commitments in a row make this introvert feel exhausted. If we're not intentional, it's easy to overbook our calendars and end up feeling depleted, emotionally and physically.

2. **Think about these practical questions:**

   · Am I fueling my body? Am I drinking enough water? Am I getting enough iron? Am I drinking too much caffeine or eating too much sugar?
   · Am I getting good, quality sleep? Am I looking at screens right before bed? Am I distracted by worries?
   · Is my space depleting my energy? Does clutter steal my energy? Am I spending too much time on my home in a way that's draining me?

   Take an inventory of these questions and experiment with changes to see if you notice a difference in your energy level.

3. **Take some deep breaths.** Shallow breathing happens naturally when we are stressed or exhausted, and when this becomes a pattern, it has a big impact on how we feel. When we intentionally take deep breaths, however, we can relieve tension, improve mental concentration, and

increase our energy. In moments when I feel myself spinning into panic mode, I try to stop and change the tempo from shallow, quick breaths to slow, deep breaths.

KEY VERSE

Those who trust in the LORD will find new strength. They will soar high on wings like eagles. They will run and not grow weary. They will walk and not faint.

ISAIAH 40:31

PRAYER

Father, you are my source of energy! Forgive me for believing the lie that part of mom life is complaining about being tired. Instead, let me see the blessing of weariness because it keeps me constantly coming back to you as my source of strength. I simply cannot do this without you. Would you also help me not to sit back and wait for a miraculous burst of energy but instead to make smart choices that will fuel this body you've given me? Make clear to me the things that deplete me, and help me to get rid of them or minimize the power they have over me. In Jesus' name, amen.

Chapter 8

WHAT'S NEXT, PAPA?

Say Hello to More Joy

I RECENTLY NOTICED an unsettling trend in our bedtime routine. I used to love spending that time with Vivi, but for a while, every time I tucked her in for the night, I wasn't in the mood to read a book. I wasn't in the mood for songs or even prayers. I just wanted to give her a kiss, tell her I loved her, and check out for the day, assuming that clocking out would bring me joy. Pretty soon it was obvious that this wasn't a fluke—it was a pattern. I couldn't keep making excuses for why I wasn't filled with joy at bedtime—like blaming sickness or a really long day —because it was happening *every* night.

I had to face the truth: I simply wasn't choosing to see the joy in those moments. Lord knows, when I do choose joy, I'm not disappointed. I feel God's goodness so wildly when bedtime isn't just another chore but a chance to soak up every new freckle on my daughter's nose or hear her say funny things I'm so glad I didn't miss. It's not bedtime that steals my joy. It's me.

If you asked me if I'm a naturally joyful person, I'd say yes. But maybe that's just wishful thinking—most of us remember our stories as if we're the great heroines, our highlight reels filled with all the times we've bucked up and had a good attitude. However, when I pull back the curtain and replay the events of the day, I have to admit that my natural tendency is to lean toward the melancholy and expect the worst. Joy is something I have to fight for.

Maybe this is you, too. Maybe the full, uncut reel of your day would reveal something that looks like this:

- You wish that your kids could fend for themselves and that you didn't have to make them *another* meal.
- You get bummed about the rain that's keeping your kids inside.
- You tick down the hours until bedtime, when you can finally get some time to yourself.
- You grab your phone hoping to be inspired but instead walk away feeling dissatisfied with life inside your four walls.

If any of these could be said of you, don't despair. Your dreary reality means there are countless moments for you to take your joy to the next level. These joy-filled moments are ripe for the picking—even for me, the melancholy girl.

So practically speaking, how can we achieve more joy? It's one thing not to be grumpy, but how can we experience Jesus-level joy? We want to do more than stay in a neutral zone. And from the little I know about science, I know that things don't really stay still. If we're drifting, we're likely to drift in a negative direction—we don't normally drift up. So we're going to need to figure out this joy stuff so we don't slip out of neutral and back into grumpy.

IN UNLIKELY PLACES

I wish I could share something really profound with you about how to find joy, but the truest answer is the most obvious one: joy is found in Jesus. More specifically, joy is found in our obedience to Jesus.

As we pursue the one true God with our whole hearts, we obey him as an act of worship. And as we obey him, we are filled with a joy that is deeper than any kind of satisfaction the world could offer.

So what does it mean, in everyday life with our kids, to have this kind of joy? It means that even when we do hard things out of obedience, we have the comfort of knowing we are choosing God's best. Deuteronomy 6:3 reminds us that our loss of joy may be a result of disobedience: "Listen closely, Israel, and be careful to obey. Then all will go well with you, and you will have many children in the land flowing with milk and honey, just as the LORD, the God of your ancestors, promised you." There are negative consequences for disobedience, so doesn't it stand to reason that obedience brings joy?

God blesses our obedience. I get all twitchy saying that, because I know it sounds like it's doused in snake oil—do what you're supposed to do, and you'll get rewarded. But I'm not saying that every person whose life looks perfect earned those blessings. And I'm not saying that everyone whose life is hard earned those negative circumstances. A call to obedience should not be taken as a call to perfection.

I got this one wrong for a long time. It has taken a storm of conversations, a lot of Bible study, many sermons, and countless books to free myself from the pressure of perfection. But I don't want to overlook the fact that sometimes we miss out on God's goodness simply because we don't obey his plan and choose to follow our own instead. And really, the biggest blessing of obedience isn't a tangible blessing at all—it's being in deeper relationship with Jesus.

At times, obedience may seem like the very thing that causes me to be grumpy. Feeling like I have to do something that isn't my plan doesn't always feel joyful in the moment. But this is part of our countercultural God—in the long term, obedience is the true path to happiness. And although our eternal destination isn't decided by how clean our record is, our obedience surely paves the way for how we walk out life here on earth with God, which is the key to our joy. Elisabeth Elliot says, "[The Lord] tells us what to do, and we find our happiness in doing it. We will not find it anywhere else. We will not find it by doing only what we want to do and not doing what we don't want to do. That is the popular idea of what freedom is, but it does not work. Freedom lies in keeping the rules. Joy is there too."[1]

One of my absolute favorite verses is Psalm 16:11: "You make known to me the path of life; in your presence there is fullness of joy; at your right hand are pleasures forevermore" (ESV). When I read this verse, I get this sweet visual of simply doing life with God and how that changes every mundane moment into a delight. What a beautiful reminder that as we seek more of God and learn to live in his presence, we'll find joy! And not just run-of-the-mill joy, but joy that the world can't fully comprehend.

In those moments from the uncut reel of your day—especially the not-so-joyful ones—are you aware of God's presence? He's always there, but at times he feels closer than at other times. For me, I'm most joyless when I'm walking unaware of his presence.

True obedience isn't a call to do the right thing all the time and achieve some kind of outward perfection. It is a heart issue that overflows into our actions. I can obey God and it can still look sloppy and imperfect. But if I'm obeying God to the fullest, I am bound to find joy, regardless of how it looks to the outside world.

LIVING EXPECTANTLY

When I was a new mom, one of the most frequent complaints I heard from other moms was about the never-ending stream of diapers. Before Vivi was born, I knew I couldn't dwell on how many thousands of diapers I would end up changing before she was potty trained. If I allowed my mind to go on that detour, I would potentially lose years of my life. Instead, I wanted to focus on the beautiful face I had the opportunity to captivate for a minute straight and the soft baby skin that always made me smile.

Just the other day, I changed the diaper of my second daughter and realized I've barely noticed the chore of diapers over the last nearly five years. This is no small thing, considering the clientele on my changing table. Vana is my spirited daughter. And by "spirited," I mean she does somersaults and shouts, "No diaper! No diaper!" every time I break out the wipes. But somehow a melancholy like me has managed to make sure motherhood is more than a depressing string of diapers and tantrums. I don't mind changing diapers the way I assumed I was destined to, and as a result, I've missed six to ten opportunities for dread every day for the past half of a decade.

Perception is everything. I didn't dread the fact I couldn't go to the bathroom alone until I heard other moms listing it among the many reasons motherhood is hard. As soon as I realized what a travesty it was that I couldn't pee alone, I started taking notice. And not just noticing, but getting annoyed with my daughters for something that a week earlier had flattered me (hey, they will travel to the ends of the world—or bedroom—to be with me!). Sometimes we lose our joy simply because of the power of suggestion.

Another area that gets me tangled up is making meals. If you start stacking up even a week's worth of breakfasts, lunches, and dinners, it begins to feel like a slippery slope. And before I send us all the way down the hill, let me assure you that there's an alternative. We can start living expectantly. We can start to see the mundane moments of the day as opportunities for hope. Instead of expecting only hard things to happen, we can see the potential that awaits us too.

When I wake up and make myself available to God's plan, knowing what a good and creative God he is, I find joy. I keep my eyes peeled for the good and forget the little things that frustrate me. I look for opportunities to serve others and connect with them. I look for what God is already doing that I can hop into.

When it comes to dinners, I might need to adjust my expectations a bit. It may be time for me to take my eyes off the meal itself and get expectant about the conversations that can happen when the four of us sit down together after a long day. Ironically, despite how much I can dread dinnertime, that's when some of my most cherished memories for our little family occur. Yes, there are tears and girls who refuse to eat their food and a sentence that gets interrupted thirty times before it's finished. But there are also moments that fill us with so much joy. Vivi says hilarious things, Vana makes the funniest faces, Tyler shares news about his day, and we laugh belly laughs. We get a chance to pray together, the girls share food, and Tyler and I share the occasional smile when we look at our sweet life.

One of my favorite passages of Scripture is Romans 8:15-17: "This resurrection life you received from God is not a timid, grave-tending life. It's adventurously expectant, greeting God with a childlike 'What's next, Papa?'" (MSG). I don't want to wake up each morning dreading what's ahead because I think I'll just be changing diapers and sitting in the carpool line and doing dishes and washing clothes. This is what the world tries to convince us motherhood is, and when we buy into this lie, it shouldn't surprise us that we become grumpy. Instead, I want to wake up each morning coming to God with adventurous expectation, asking, "What's next, Papa?"

We can find joy when we focus on *who* is a part of our day instead of *what* we will do.

JOY IN THE MUNDANE

I spent a solid three days in Waco at Magnolia's Spring at the Silos selling our journals at the vendor market. My team and I got to hear from many of our current customers about how our products have played a role in deepening their faith and growing their prayer life. On the drive home, I felt like I was in limbo—feeling elated from this incredible high but nervous about what it would look like to return to everyday life. I was afraid of being disappointed when things got back to normal and I returned to all the mundane tasks that make up most of my days.

The day after I got back, I went to Target with the girls.

They were being silly and singing, just bursting with joy. As we checked out, they brought smiles to everyone around our cart. I didn't have "Make a difference at Target" on my list for the day, but that moment put my fears to rest. It put a stop to the lie that the small life is somehow not as joyful as doing big things for Jesus. The small things are definitely less flashy and harder to spot, but they're there if we look for them.

The problem is that we can't always plan for life-giving moments like this one. I think that's why we try to measure our level of joy by what's ahead on the calendar. We can look forward to a vacation, but we're solemn and bored when it comes to a standard Tuesday. But God isn't boring, and even though we can't stop doing all the mundane things that might bring us dread, we can invite him to be a part of our lives—including the ordinary tasks. We can ask, "What's next, Papa?" and allow him to change the way we see our sometimes-small lives.

I am learning that true joy is not found in any of the places the world tells us to look. Not in sleep. Not in good kids. Not in easy days. Not in perfect meals and clean homes. Not in adventure itself. The fullness of joy is found only in the Lord.

We don't default to joy. We have to fight for it. Scripture gives us this rather surprising command about joy: "Always be joyful" (1 Thessalonians 5:16). At first that sounds impossible, but when we recognize that Jesus is walking beside us through every part of our day, it gives us the perspective we need in order to see everything as a way to serve him. Even if it means changing the twelfth diaper today and not going to the bathroom in peace for several weeks running.

ACTION STEPS

1. **Recognize that someone wants what you're complaining about.** Frankly, I hate this advice. I hate to be cut off when I'm trying to be bummed about something, but it's true all the same. My desire to feel validated and my attempt to prove that my situation is harder than someone else's does nothing good for me. Believe it or not, there are women out there who would beg to be in your shoes and be overwhelmed by #momlife.

2. **Know your valleys.** Write down the lowest moments of your day. Do you notice any trends that send you into a downward spiral? When you know what your triggers are, it's easier to be proactive. What verses or prayers can help you refocus when you find yourself in a valley?

3. **Never forget who gave you the blessings in the first place.** Deuteronomy 8:11-14 says, "Beware that in your plenty you do not forget the LORD your God and disobey his commands, regulations, and decrees that I am giving you today. For when you have become full and prosperous and have built fine homes to live in, and when your flocks and herds have become very large and your silver and gold have multiplied along with everything else, be careful! Do not become proud at that time and forget the LORD your God, who rescued you from slavery." Sometimes our blessings give us spiritual amnesia. Make it a daily habit to thank God for all he's given you.

KEY VERSE

You make known to me the path of life; in your presence there is fullness of joy; at your right hand are pleasures forevermore.

PSALM 16:11, ESV

PRAYER

Father, it is so exciting to live with the fullness of your joy, but many days I feel like my minute-by-minute circumstances try to convince me that joy isn't possible. Help me to reject this lie. I've given my circumstances too much power, so now I transfer that power from my circumstances to you. Please remove all thoughts of discouragement, bitterness, and comparison. Instead, give me a heart of gratitude and eyes to notice every blessing in front of me. In Jesus' name, amen.

PART THREE

DEVELOP

Chapter 9

ROUGH EDGES

Say Hello to Refinement

IT WAS A SLEEPLESS WEEK WITH our eight-month-old. After being spoiled with ten-plus-hour stretches at night for the preceding five months, it felt like a rude awakening. I expected the lack of sleep in the beginning. But now? I was just frustrated.

I racked my brain trying to fix the problem. Was Vana teething? Was she having a growth spurt? Was she hungry? Essentially, I was trying to fix her. Then God brought to mind something I heard a pastor say years ago. He reminded me that many times what we see as the problem is not what the Lord sees as the problem. Perhaps the Lord wasn't trying to solve the problem of the not-so-sleepy Vana. Maybe he was trying to work on the heart of the too-easily-angered Valerie.

Every unrefined area in motherhood represents a prime opportunity for us to change, even when we think the attention should be on our kids' rough edges. It's hard to admit that

I'm the problem. I see these glaring missteps in the people I love and wonder why God would use something so enormous to chip away at the ittiest, bittiest rough spots in me. Surely my need to learn patience or to give my family grace wouldn't warrant all *this*.

That's my version, anyway.

I tried to back off of the idea that I needed to figure out the cause of Vana's sleeplessness and instead tried to hear what God was teaching me. I was no longer approaching the situation like a blacksmith trying to beat out a piece of metal. Instead, I wanted to be open to the possibility that I am not, in fact, perfect and that maybe God was using this to transform *me*.

The hiccups in parenting aren't just things that push my buttons. They're opportunities for me to grow. Just as I long to rub out the rough spots in my kids to help them become the people God wants them to be, God is doing the same thing with me.

This whole motherhood thing is quite the process, isn't it? If I didn't have motherhood to smooth out all these rough edges, God would use something else to chip away at me. I prefer this method—it comes with cuddles and giggles and footie pajamas.

Sometimes the chipping away is so painful that I forget God isn't cutting away the core of me; he's sloughing off the dead skin like a pumice stone does. It may hurt, but it's for my own good. I tend to assume that every trial is part of the devil's plan to sabotage me and make my life miserable, but in reality, God may be trying to grow something good in me.

The cliché of motherhood is that we are either perfect or an absolute mess—there is nothing in between. But maybe the reality looks more like this: we're sometimes-messy mommas who are being refined into God's image. I much prefer that description.

THE BEST QUALITY EVER

Solomon was the third king of Israel—the son of King David. When he became king, God told him he could ask for anything (see 2 Chronicles 1:7). Solomon could have asked for power or fame or wealth, but instead, this is what he asked for:

> Give me now wisdom and knowledge, that I may go out and come in before this people, for who can rule this great people of Yours?
> 2 CHRONICLES 1:10, NASB

Doesn't this response show how wise Solomon already was? Of all the immediate fixes he could have requested, the guy prayed for wisdom. I would have asked for help with my laundry.

Here was God's response to Solomon's request:

> Because your greatest desire is to help your people, and you did not ask for wealth, riches, fame, or even the death of your enemies or a long life, but rather you asked for wisdom and knowledge to properly govern my people—I will certainly give you the wisdom and knowledge you requested.
> 2 CHRONICLES 1:11-12

God wants us to ask for wisdom. How lavishly God blessed Solomon when he asked for it!

This seems pretty obvious to me now, but somehow I'd never really thought to ask God what he wanted to develop in me. I assumed that I didn't need to seek it out—that he would just tell me. But ever since I started asking him how he wants me to grow, he has been speaking to me so clearly. I'm starting to recognize weaknesses that I never recognized as weaknesses before. This is much better than my old method of fumbling around from mistake to mistake, wondering what God was trying to teach me. God had to shout to get my attention, and the cost was higher.

Believe me, this refinement process can still be messy, but it feels a bit more intentional and proactive now. Case in point: I recognize my struggle to put down my phone before my toddler's meltdown calls my attention to it.

I have also found that I'm wasting less time in denial about my weaknesses. I figure if I'm going to ask a question, I should probably be open to an answer. There's no point in asking God what he wants to refine in me if I'm hoping he'll just say, "Oh Val, you're actually way ahead of the game." When I submit myself to his refining, I am well aware that there is soul scrubbing to be done. And while this process doesn't come without some scrapes, I no longer pour salt into the wound by pretending to be squeaky clean (which always seems to double the time it takes me to learn the lessons the Lord has for me).

Solomon was really on to something—a teachable spirit is worth its weight in gold. If we stay open to the idea that there's work to be done in us, not just in those around us, we can be radically transformed. We don't have to be destined to become stubborn old curmudgeons who can't embrace change or criticism.

If you are frustrated that you yell at your kids or you're afraid that your kids will only remember you cleaning or working or spending time on your phone, take courage. This doesn't have to be your story. We have a gracious God. Philippians 1:6 says, "I am certain that God, who began the good work within you, will continue his work until it is finally finished on the day when Christ Jesus returns." There is no limit to who we can become if we are willing to let God rough us up a little bit and cultivate something new in us.

THE SPOTLIGHT BURNS

One of the most humbling experiences as a parent is that moment when your kid calls you out for losing your cool. Not three hours ago, Vivi told me to "take a breath." This is the advice I give to her when she's in a tizzy, and I wasn't expecting to hear it boomerang back to me. Apparently I was in a tizzy in that moment too.

I want my girls to think I'm Superwoman, but I'm far from it. So when a spotlight is directed at my imperfections, this is the truth I have to focus on: my rough edges are the very things God is using to grow my kids.

It's true—all that brokenness has exponential benefits. Our kids get a front-row seat to what God can do with our messes. And although it sounds scary and we fear we might screw up our kids royally, God has a purpose even in our imperfections. Can you imagine having a perfect momma and how intimidating that would be? How could you learn the beauty of forgiveness and fall in love with a God who rescues us from ourselves? How could you learn grace and that God longs for our hearts, not for spotlessness? How could you believe that our ticket to heaven isn't the result of our works but is a free gift from God?

Psalm 66:8-12 says, "Praise our God, all peoples, let the sound of his praise be heard; he has preserved our lives and kept our feet from slipping. For you, God, tested us; you refined us like silver. You brought us into prison and laid burdens on our backs. You let people ride over our heads; we went through fire and water, but you brought us to a place of abundance" (NIV). The writer's source of abundance came through prison and testing and fire and water. The very things that preserved his life were things we typically don't identify with blessing. Maybe the things in your life that you think will kill you or at least steal your spirit will actually bring abundant life. This passage proves that God's equations are better than my worldly math. In these verses, prisons and burdens equal abundance.

Lara Casey puts it this way in her book *Cultivate*: "We dismiss the dirt and the mess as bad, trying to keep it off our hands and out of our homes. But dirt holds a certain magic, cradling new life. Your past mistakes, your heartache, your circumstances, and the tension you feel right now in your season—every bit of it is part of your growing ground."[1] As someone who is naturally wired to like order, I find this challenging. There will never be a day when I see letting dirt into my house as a good thing, and I instinctually feel the same way about the mistakes and messes I make. So this is going to require a big mind shift. But when we can accept that God's refinement is going to be a little messy, we'll be able to fully embrace the way God wants to transform us through motherhood.

It's time to let go of the idea that someone more perfect than you could do a better job raising your kids. God picked you—and not the heavenly, sanctified version of you. The real you, who is late to school even when you try your hardest to get there on time. The one who forgets to brush her kids' teeth or feed them a meal with all the food groups represented. The one who says foolish things. The one who is still learning to let her four-year-old get the last piece of dessert. (Or is that just me?)

If you long to see your kids apologize with humbleness and repent of their sin, they have to see it modeled for them. And guess what? You are their biggest influence. So if they are seeing refinement happen in you, rejoice! The things that plague you most are the very things God can use to show your kids what grace looks like.

BEFORE THINGS GET SLOPPY

You can't spend more than five minutes online or chatting with a group of friends before you come across one of the most common stereotypes about motherhood: the "hot-mess mom." I'll tread lightly here, because we have all no doubt used this phrase at some point, myself included. It sounds harmless, and we often say it in an effort to commiserate or find common ground. But when we start believing the lie that being a big mess is part of our identity, it can become a life sentence. We start making blanket assumptions like these:

- With a newborn, it's impossible to think clearly. (Believe me, I think there really is such a thing as mommy brain, but we don't have to wallow in that mess.)
- With five kids, there's no way I can be a good friend.
- I'll be less of a hot mess when the kids are grown, I promise.

This is not to say that life doesn't have hot-mess moments or times when things get out of control. But we don't have to be victims to this definition of motherhood. As soon as we start thinking this is the extent of who we are or that we are helpless to do anything to change our circumstances, we lose all hope. And although it's true that some things are out of our control, we do have control over the way we respond to these things. It's time we stopped saying something is impossible if God never said it was.

ACTION STEPS

1. **Ask the Lord what he wants to refine in you during this season.** Be on the lookout for how he speaks to you. Does a topic keep coming up in Scripture or in sermons? Are you starting to become sensitive to something you never noticed before, like a sharp tone in your voice or a thought that tends to creep in that never really bothered you before? Let the Lord work in that area through prayer, and see how you can take action too.

2. **Model repentance.** When you make a mistake, apologize to your kids and ask for their forgiveness. Let them see the refining process in action.

3. **Refuse to call yourself and others a hot mess.** The next time you hear someone talking about how all mommas are a hot mess, change the direction of the conversation and compliment her on some area she is flourishing in.

KEY VERSE

For you, God, tested us; you refined us like silver.
PSALM 66:10, NIV

PRAYER

Father, I am eternally grateful that you aren't done with me yet! Please continue to refine me. When I am butting heads with my kids, remind me that you are smoothing out my rough edges. What a privilege that this hard process comes with giggles and cuddles. In Jesus' name, amen.

Chapter 10

MOTHERHOOD ISN'T YOUR SAFETY NET

Say Hello to Undelayed Dreams

IT HAS BEEN AT LEAST FIFTEEN YEARS since I saw *The Shawshank Redemption*, but all these years later, there's a scene that still haunts me. It's near the end of the movie, when Morgan Freeman's character is released from prison, and he finds it difficult to handle the freedom. After being confined for so long, he almost prefers the comforts of prison.

As moms, we know the work we do at home can be really hard. We're "on" all the time—there's no escaping it. But at some point, we might be given an opportunity to do something beyond our four walls. As exhilarating as that sounds, the freedom of dreaming can also be more uncomfortable than what we know what to do with. As much as motherhood can box us in, sometimes we like the security it offers. The security of dirty diapers and crumb-covered floors. The security of sibling squabbles and dirty hair. We feel safe here because we know how things work—we don't have to stretch outside our comfort zones.

I hear the irony of this. But this is a reality for a lot of us.

Almost from the moment we become moms, we start feeling pressure—whether it's from our community or our church or within ourselves—to sacrifice every dream and calling for the sake of our kids. And yes, there are definitely sacrifices God calls us to make on behalf of our children. But sometimes we use our role as moms as an excuse not to do what God is calling us to do. It might sound selfless and loving to forgo using our gifts and talents, but this isn't a biblical kind of selflessness; it's a crutch that prevents us from leaving the comfort of our four crayon-stained walls.

This conversation isn't really about whether we stay at home or work outside the home or work part time or work from home or do some combination of the above. The reality is that God calls each mom to a unique situation, and this may look different in different seasons. The point is that we can't stay stuck in what's safe if God is calling us to something outside our comfort zones.

Regardless of our work situation, it's possible to hide behind motherhood and let it swallow up God's call on us to be anything besides moms. He might be calling you to mentor young women, work a desk job, run a business, or volunteer for a nonprofit.

Have you been feeling a tug on your heart to do something with your gifts during this season? Have you been pushing back that voice that's prompting you to join the project, write the blog, or start the business—all because you think it has to wait until your kids are grown? We can't sidestep our callings from God just because we're in the middle of raising kids.

WHY WE SAY NO

When I dig deeper into my typical reasons for saying no to things God may be nudging me to do, I realize how often I use my kids as an excuse. Here are a few recent examples:

- I can't go to that church event because I can't be away for bedtime. *Truth: If I tried, I could find someone to watch the kids. And once I'm out the door, my kids will adjust. The real reason is that I'm terrified of being called on or just not in the mood to talk to others.*
- I can't go on a mission trip and be away from my family. *Truth: I'm afraid of visiting a country in poverty and being without my comforts. Plain and simple.*
- I can't volunteer with the refugee ministry because we're too busy. *Truth: I could find something I can do that works with our family. The real reason I don't volunteer is I don't like committing to things.*

What's driving my no in these situations is fear, not my kids, despite what I tell people (and what I often tell myself). I'm embarrassed by how easily I can use my kids to justify my own wants. Living this way, with an air of self-preservation and a boatload of excuses, only fuels Grumpy Mom. When we aren't living out our God-given purpose, nothing will satisfy us. We can try to live comfortable lives, free from being stretched or experiencing pain, but it will always leave us wanting.

I have to wonder if this is, in fact, the very reason motherhood lets us down sometimes. We've put all our hopes and dreams in a particular life stage, when in reality, God wants us to step out in faith and follow his call for us in the midst of motherhood.

WHEN LIFE GETS BORING

A few months ago, I told my life coach that life just felt really mundane. From the outside looking in, I was doing some pretty cool things, but it was all in my comfort zone. I felt bad admitting that our beautiful but routine life felt super boring. Does any mom want to admit that? The result was a lot of tension and frustration over the littlest things my girls did. I was the definition of a grumpy mom. And then something happened that completely changed my perspective.

My boring life took a quick turn to anything but boring. God has a sense of humor, doesn't he?

First, let me set the scene for you. My two biggest fears are flying and speaking in groups. On that particular day, I was facing three situations that pushed all my fear buttons: (1) I'd started a business mastermind, and now I was on the hook for speaking in front of them *and* having to fly in a plane to get there, (2) there was a mission trip to Haiti I wanted to go on (insert flying over an ocean), which was bringing up the additional fear of leaving my comfort zone, and (3) my pastor had asked me to speak at church on Mother's Day because my husband happened to drop something about this book on motherhood.

Want to know my first thought about all these "non-boring" events? Fear, obviously. In the span of less than a week, all these situations piled up, and I had to face an enormous fear sandwich.

My second thought: *Can I just make a DIY headboard?*

I am not kidding. I was so desperate to avoid my fears that I tried to find solace in DIYing. And if you talk to me for half a minute, you know I don't DIY. But even a task I'd previously dreaded felt like a welcome distraction from what I feared more. This is my version of nest life. What's yours? When dreams get hard and things get a little scary, the nest life feels safe. We can DIY to God's glory, if that's what we're called to do. The question is, are we acting from a deep conviction in our souls, or are we acting out of fear?

I finally got on that plane a few days later. I was afraid to the point of tears as I hugged my girls goodbye and prepared to board. I wanted my four walls more than ever. Those first ten minutes on the plane were panic filled, but as we lifted off, I was surprised to find that my ears could safely reach an altitude of thirty thousand feet without bursting. I felt the joy of going beyond what I thought I was capable of. The world was now my oyster.

Those days away changed me. I conquered two fears, and I got to reap the benefit of what lay just beyond it. Being able to hop on a plane, be inspired by fellow business owners, and return to my family just days later refreshed and inspired me. I came back a different mom. I can't fully explain it, but the proof is in the pudding. I came back with more grace for my kids, more joy for their stories, more patience for the hard parts, and more willingness to serve.

Had I chosen to DIY a headboard (which I hope will eventually happen) out of pure fear and a desire to avoid God's call, I have no doubt that my frustrations would have continued. Because when we say no to God, it will frustrate every other aspect of our lives.

WHAT ARE WE CAPABLE OF?

When I take myself out of a race God has called me to, it's usually because I'm picturing running without him. God is capable of doing so much more than we think is possible. Without God's perspective, we will decide what we can and can't do based on our own strength. This flies in the face of Ephesians 3:20, which says that God "is able to do far more abundantly than all that we ask or think, according to the power at work within us" (ESV).

In other words, what he has planned is better.

I'm a goal setter to the nth degree. I love dreaming and making plans, but even I can't dream up plans that come close to what God has in mind. No matter how big of a dreamer you are, God is bigger. Does that mean that if you dream of four kids, God is dreaming of eleven, or if you dream of making $50,000 a year, he is dreaming of $100,000? Not necessarily. Bigger isn't always measured the way we think, but it's always *greater*.

I love how God paints the picture of doing something greater in the life of Moses. God called him to do something—you know, confront Pharaoh and lead two million or so grumblers and complainers through the desert—and he responded with a laundry list of excuses, including a fear that's near and dear to one of my own: "O Lord, I'm not very good with words. I never have been, and I'm not now, even though you have spoken to me. I get tongue-tied, and my words get tangled" (Exodus 4:10). As someone who is equally terrified of speaking in front of people, I'm grateful for the Lord's response to Moses. Despite Moses' excuses, God was gracious and sent Moses' eloquent brother, Aaron, with him. This story reminds me of a few things when it comes to God's dreams for us:

- **God has a great desire for us to be a part of his plan.** Can he do it without us? Yes! Does he long to use us anyway? Yes! We can make excuses, but God will still pursue us.
- **We don't accomplish God's purposes alone.** Moses' weakness meant that both he and Aaron got to be part of the story. Shake off the feeling that God expects you

to do it all. Maybe God is surrounding you with some of his other kids so they can use their gifts and so you can carry out the mission together.

· **He equips each of us differently.** Your calling from God might look very different from your friend's or your neighbor's or your sister's. Maybe your gift is in leading Bible studies or volunteering for outreaches or cooking meals or organizing details behind the scenes. Moses had the words, while Aaron was the good talker. Each gift is equally important in God's eyes.

· **When God says we're the ones for the job, we have to banish the idea that someone else would be a better fit.** Moses couldn't believe that he was the right man for the job—he kept insisting there was someone better. But God was relentless in his assertion that Moses was the one to do it.

Ephesians 2:10 says, "We are His workmanship [His own master work, a work of art], created in Christ Jesus [reborn from above—spiritually transformed, renewed, ready to be used] for good works, which God prepared [for us] beforehand [taking paths which He set], so that we would walk in them [living the good life which He prearranged and made ready for us]" (AMP). You and I are ready to be used! God isn't waiting for us to become perfect or free from responsibilities or free from diapers or free from having kids at home. He is ready to use us now.

So get after it, momma! Live out the call God has for you.

FOREVER WAITING ON THE LORD

You might be thinking, *I've never rejected something God told me to do!* But there are ways we can frustrate God's plans without blatantly saying no. James 4:17 says, "It is sin to know what you ought to do and then not do it." Sometimes we know what God has called us to do, but out of fear or insecurity or self-doubt, we push that calling to the back burner. And sometimes our excuse is that we are "waiting to hear from God." I imagine we have all done this at some point. We hear a prompting from the Lord, but we want a louder one. We sense that God is nudging us, but we want it written in the sky. We want our marching orders to land on our front door. But our God is a God of both thunderclaps and a gentle wind. Our call may come in a faint whisper, without the fanfare we're waiting for.

Maybe you've heard the story about Gideon and how he put out a fleece. He asked God to make the fleece wet or dry to confirm what God was asking him to do. This wasn't as cute as it sounds, because it showed Gideon's lack of faith. Gideon already had God's direction. He told God in Judges 6:37, "I will put a wool fleece on the threshing floor tonight. If the fleece is wet with dew in the morning but the ground is dry, then I will know that you are going to help me rescue Israel *as you promised*" (emphasis added). God was still faithful, despite Gideon's doubt, but I have to wonder how this story would have been different if Gideon had taken God at his word.

Maybe the fleece you are waiting on is that your calling will feel comfortable. I hate to break the news, but that's not a sign God commonly gives. Don't I wish! I'm a big believer that we have to take the first step before we feel comfortable. I had to get on a plane before I was at peace with it. Peter had to get out of the boat before he found out he wouldn't sink (Matthew 14). Noah had to build the ark before it started raining (Genesis 6). We don't obey blindly, but with faith in who God is and who we have known him to be in the past.

Are there things God has put on your heart to do, but you've been waiting for big signs before you pursue them? Maybe there are no billboards telling you what to do, but when you look back at the details, you see God connecting the pieces and providing the opportunities. I'm not saying that we should make our new default answer yes. It's entirely possible to swing in the other direction and assume that God always wants us to do the scariest, most uncomfortable thing. We should have no default at all and instead follow the Holy Spirit. Sure, we need plans and boundaries, but we don't need to hold on to them so tightly that they keep us from following the Lord's promptings.

Have you been believing the lie that because you're a mom, all other dreams are off the table? If so, I want to encourage you to live a life that is surrendered to the Lord, bringing all opportunities before him and then obeying as soon as you get direction from him. When we're flying with Jesus, he is the only safety net we'll need.

ACTION STEPS

1. **Just start.** God prepared good works for you to do today. You might not have a big plan mapped out, but start right where you are and keep your eyes open. God calls us to be faithful with the small things, and who knows—these little things might be preparing us for bigger things ahead.

2. **Set your eyes on eternity.** If your eyes are focused on eternity, it will change the decisions you make. Are you fixated on things that don't offer eternal value? Are there distractions that hold you back from your Kingdom-led mission here on earth?

3. **Take your kids with you.** Whenever you can, include your kids in your calling, whether that's physically or just conversationally. I long to teach my kids how to love others selflessly and not be so focused on themselves. What better way to do that than by having them see me serve others and share the journey with them?

KEY VERSE

All glory to God, who is able, through his mighty power at work within us, to accomplish infinitely more than we might ask or think.

EPHESIANS 3:20

PRAYER

Father, give me clarity for what you are calling me to do with this season of my life. Remove any fear and lies that have kept me from the mission you have for me. If I haven't been receptive to your prompting in the past, make me open to the possibility that you long to use me in some capacity. And for the things I already know you want me to do, give me courage to step out in obedience. In Jesus' name, amen.

Chapter 11

IT'S TEMPORARY

Say Hello to Embracing Each Season

I DO THIS SILLY THING when something out of our comfortable routine happens two or three times in a row: I immediately ball up on the floor and resign myself to the fact that this is just how life is now. Three days in a row of teething, and I decide that sleep is gone forever. Three days of a picky eater, and all of a sudden I'm convinced my child will never eat again. I am so quick to forget how seasonal life is.

As moms, we see seasons change often as our kids develop and as school years start and end, yet we still stress over the infant who wakes up every two hours or the never-ending dirty diapers or the seemingly bottomless laundry basket. In the thick of motherhood, we need to be reminded that life is a series of seasons and that is actually a beautiful thing.

It seems like we can swing to one extreme or the other

when it comes to the seasons of motherhood: *This will never end* or *I wish this could last forever.*

Neither of these mind-sets brings us freedom or echoes the truth of Scripture. That means they both have the potential to take us down a negative road.

THE NECESSITY OF SEASONS

Let's start with some high-level truths about seasons. The highest level. That's right—I'm talking all the way up to heaven.

When we start thinking that this will never end, we need to remember that this tough season won't last forever. Praise the Lord! Only heaven will.

When we start wishing we could stay in this season, we need to remember that this good season won't last forever. Praise the Lord! Heaven is even better!

Join me back here on earth and tell me: Do you crave each season like I do? I'd say that fall is my favorite, but the truth is, I enjoy each one. After a long winter, I'm yearning for that first sunny morning that chases away my winter blues. After a refreshing spring, I'm ready for fun by the pool. And after a hot summer, I'm excited for fall, when all the neighborhood kids play together and friends come over for dinner on our porch under the bistro lights. And after a full fall, I'm ready for the coziness of cold days and hot gumbo.

As much as this South Louisiana girl may dream of California weather and consistently perfect temperatures sometimes, I really do love having four distinct seasons. And from what I've heard, although Californians love their weather, they actually wouldn't mind a little variety. My humidity-frizzed hair doesn't get it, but my heart does.

As you know by now, I've been the mom bored with a

beautiful but flatlined life. The circumstances I was bored with after a long period of sameness were the very things that I was so grateful for after a really rough season for our family. The valleys and mountaintops give us perspective we wouldn't otherwise have from a life lived on the plateaus.

EXPANDING YOUR CAPACITY

Some seasons are challenging because they require more capacity than we think we have. A newborn in the house, our firstborn starting college, our lastborn starting kindergarten—those life changes can feel overwhelming, and we may feel like we aren't cut out for them. But there is purpose in the ebb and flow of seasons—they're not just there to yank us around and make us feel like we're on a roller coaster. Without the stretching and pulling, we wouldn't be able to expand the capacity of what we can handle. Every season that feels like too much is part of the sanctifying process.

This girl who craves margin has been in a doozy of a season. It's been a really good one, but way fuller than I'm used to. At the same time I was nearing the deadline for this book, I got the opportunity to go to my dream event—Magnolia Market's Spring at the Silos. When I got the offer, I was thrilled. But I also knew this would be a challenge. Thankfully this would only be for a season, otherwise I no doubt would have given up several times.

Being the giant nerd that I am, I decided that if I was going to Waco, I needed to study up. So I pulled out *The Magnolia Story*, which had been waiting for me on my bookshelf, and started to read. Joanna and Chip share their story on these pages, and it's quite the adventure, but I never expected this book to change me. Threaded throughout their story, I kept noticing the theme of capacity. At one point Joanna says that she told herself, "If I wanted to do important work one day, I would have to increase my capacity."[1]

Capacity. God used her words to strike a chord in my heart. I had been living every day limited by what I thought was my capacity, but what if God wanted to expand me beyond what I thought my limits were? I'm the girl who gives up when I'm tired. I'm the girl who calls for help as soon as I get stuck. I'm the girl who stops right when I think I'm at my end. I find it ironic that my name, Valerie, means "strong." It isn't natural for me to push past hard things, and I've often felt weak. But maybe my name is actually a God thing, because it reminds me that God is stretching me.

Are you in a season of getting stretched right now? If so, know that the you in ten years or even ten months will be grateful for the growth that's happening in this very moment. Jim Loehr and Tony Schwartz, in *The Power of Full Engagement*, say, "We grow at all levels by expending energy beyond our ordinary limits and then recovering." They go on to say that this stretching must be followed by adequate recovery, but "too much recovery without sufficient stress leads to atrophy and weakness."[2]

For years, I haven't willingly gone beyond what I thought was my capacity. When I got married at twenty-six, I passed off a lot of things to my husband and stopped attempting things I wasn't good at. My sister and I are twins, and she was single for an extra six years. I think that's why she knows how to hook up a router, assemble IKEA furniture, and change a tire. She stretched her capacity to learn things my muscles have been shrinking at.

It was an all-too-tangible reminder about an assumption I've made: that it was too much stress that was wounding me.

But in trying to keep every ounce of stress out, I was actually stunting my growth.

The idea of stretching our capacity is basically the modern-day lingo for what the Bible calls character-building perseverance: "We also glory in our sufferings, because we know that suffering produces perseverance; perseverance, character; and character, hope. And hope does not put us to shame, because God's love has been poured out into our hearts through the Holy Spirit, who has been given to us" (Romans 5:3-5, NIV).

Can I tell y'all how much it has freed me to learn that a little stress is actually good and will grow me? Over the last six weeks, I've had many moments when I've had to remember that my capacity is not immovable. This has enabled me to fold one more load of laundry instead of collapsing onto the sofa in the evening. It has helped me keep a good attitude when there was a lot on my plate. It has allowed me not only to bear the things I was carrying but to grin through it too.

When I accomplish what I didn't think was possible, I'm able to send Grumpy Mom out the back door. Not because I'm Superwoman, but because I'm operating purely out of the strength of the Lord. I know I'm not capable on my own, so anything beyond my own capacity reminds me how much I'm dependent on him. The promise that "when I am weak, then I am strong" (2 Corinthians 12:10) comes to life in these moments.

Maybe you thought you weren't a patient person, but waiting for your house to sell has taught you a new level of dependence on the Lord. That dependence will directly benefit every person that will one day require your patience, including those kids of yours. Maybe you didn't think you would be able to handle being in charge of the work project, but the experience of balancing a houseful of personalities as a mom has helped you manage the differing personalities on the job.

I remember being so discouraged when I found out that Vivi had flipped to a breech position just nine days before her due date. My dreams for her birth were now replaced with plans for a C-section. I was disappointed at the time, but as I look back on that season now, I can see that the recovery process required me to ask for help—something that can be a struggle for me. Thanks to that experience and the way it forced me to rely on others in a whole new way, I'm more comfortable accepting help when I need it.

FOR A SEASON

As we ponder what it means to go beyond what we think is possible in our particular seasons, we need to be careful not to swing too far in the other direction. This doesn't mean we're limitless like the one and only God. We need to recognize what is healthy stretching and what is leading us on a path toward burnout.

Not all seasons begin and end naturally. Some need our prompting, which is hopefully prompted by the Holy Spirit. There are times when we need to proactively shift our commitments so we don't get burned out. For me, that means lots of downtime after a book deadline and at times even a sabbatical with my family in the woods.

No matter what season comes our way, I want to stand on this verse: "He will be like a tree firmly planted by streams of water, which yields its fruit in its season and its leaf does not wither; and in whatever he does, he prospers" (Psalm 1:3, NASB). The beauty of this image is in where the tree is planted. It's right by the streams of nourishment. For us as believers, that means walking with the Lord and seeking him first in all we do. That tree by the stream's edge has a constant supply of water through roots that are firmly planted. It's strong and stable, which means it can withstand the elements, and it produces fruit at just the right time. I want that to be said of us in all seasons—that we are stable and strong.

This is possible, not because of our own stability and strength, but because God never changes. In the ups and downs of life, we can hold on to him. When everything around us is changing, he remains the same. James 1:17 says, "Every good and perfect gift is from above, coming down from the Father of the heavenly lights, who does not change like shifting shadows" (NIV). As we face seasons that seem to change on a dime (and without our permission), we can find comfort in a God who isn't shifty but is our firm foundation.

BALANCE IS POSSIBLE

It's easy to get so distracted by the everyday parts of motherhood that we forget it actually stretches our capacities in transformative ways. When we're in the thick of a really hard season, it can be difficult to remember that those challenges are what shape us into who we are becoming. I want to be a loud voice cheering you on right now, letting you know that whatever is most difficult in this season is going to spring up new fruit that would otherwise never grow.

Before I had kids, I was sure I would be the mom who had it all. I heard other moms talking about putting things they wanted on the back burner, and to me that sounded a lot like giving up. I mentioned in chapter 10 how fear can stunt us from following God's call on our lives, but sometimes God calls mommas to table their dreams for a season. What I saw as giving up was actually embracing a particular season. To use a gardening analogy, this is being patient for summer instead of demanding watermelons in the dead of winter.

Life is a series of shifts. Overall, I may live a balanced life, but each season has stronger pulls to different things. For a period of time, you may have a busy work season and less time at home. Then your season might shift when your big project is done. Your work calms down so your home life can be your main focus.

Do whatever you're called to in this season, and do it well, because it likely won't be the singular priority in every season. We don't want to complain our way through mountaintop experiences only to head into a valley and wish we'd enjoyed the previous season more. When we focus on being present, we can embrace each season as it comes and let it serve its purpose in our life.

Let's end this chapter with the perfect quote from Lara Casey's book *Cultivate*: "Now, embracing your season doesn't mean you have to love it; it simply means letting it be. The word amen offered at the end of a prayer means 'let it be.' In whatever season you're in, and when the new one comes, practice saying, Amen, Lord. Let it be."[3]

ACTION STEPS

1. **Identify your season.** Is this a season of stretching or resting? Is this a season of serving or accepting help? Identify what season you're in, and embrace it.

2. **Be a season ambassador.** Find ways to embrace the season you're in, and enjoy each one to the fullest. When your family complains about a rainy month, put on your raincoats and jump in puddles together, or make a warm

pot of soup together. These tangible celebrations will help you live in the present season instead of waiting for the next one.

3. **Document what you learn in each season.** I have a journal for each of my girls to document some of the significant memories throughout their childhood. After I write in each, I feel lighter, knowing I don't have to stress about each season ending. I love being able to look back and fondly remember past seasons without feeling the burden to repeat them.

KEY VERSE

They are like trees planted along the riverbank, bearing fruit each season. Their leaves never wither, and they prosper in all they do.

PSALM 1:3

PRAYER

Father, forgive me for wishing away this season in my longing for a different one. I know that without the changing seasons, there would be no fruit. Root me firmly in you, because although the seasons change, you never do. Help me to believe that you have a purpose for every season. I want to be like a tree planted along the riverbank, sturdy and unwavering, whether I'm in the midst of a sun-scorching summer or a cold, bleak winter. Give me eyes to see the good in each season. In Jesus' name, amen.

Chapter 12

LIGHTEN YOUR LOAD

Say Hello to Freedom from Guilt

I'VE ALWAYS BEEN A GOOD GIRL who valued obedience over grace. When I was a teenager in youth group, I never paid much attention to the lessons on grace. I didn't think I really needed it. I didn't have trouble doing what I thought was right, so I just stuck with that as my pathway to heaven. I figured I'd try to get to heaven by way of deeds first, and if I messed up too much, I could get there on the back roads—by way of grace. I "selflessly" saved grace for those bad girls while I did my best to get life right.

But then I had children, and heaven help me, motherhood did me in. There was no way I could rationalize that I was still on that first road. I fell—and I fell hard. My sweet little darlings can sure bring out the worst in me. Some days I yell loud enough to outscream my toddler, just so she knows who's in charge. There's nothing like having tiny human beings serve as your mirror to remind you that perfection is impossible, humanly speaking.

Motherhood unloads on us a whole new world of responsibility, and along with it comes guilt. We bear the burden not just of our parenting mistakes but of our kids' mistakes too. The world puts pressure on us to question every decision we make for our children. Should you have gone with a private school? Should you have avoided the shots? Should you have breast-fed longer? That's a lot to carry on our dainty little shoulders.

Grumpy Mom acknowledges this sense of failure, but the problem is that she stops short of embracing God's grace. She's consumed with her faults, keeping her eyes on herself instead of on God. Here's the truth: we *are* absolute screwups, but thank God, that isn't how he sees us. We have a story of redemption. As believers, we can say goodbye to mommy guilt. When it starts to fester, we can recognize it and then regroup, renewing our minds so we can live free from the negative thoughts that would otherwise sink us.

WHAT TOBYMAC TAUGHT ME ABOUT GRACE

In all my failings, motherhood has forced me to embrace a grace that goes beyond the theoretical idea you're taught in Sunday school. When you discover this concept at the ripe old age of thirty, it looks a little different than it did when you were seven. You realize the depth of your own mess. You've had a lot more opportunities to break things, or worse, to break people's spirits. You've had more opportunities to criticize, cuss, choose selfishness, act spoiled, be lazy, or willfully disobey.

You know the old sentiment "I knew everything when I was younger"? I like John Wesley's version better: "When I was young, I was sure of everything; in a few years, having been mistaken a thousand times, I was not half so sure of most things as I was before. At present I am hardly sure of anything but what God has revealed to man."[1]

This is me. I've never felt like more of a sinner. When the light of motherhood shines on me like a spotlight in an interrogation room, I realize I'm the guilty one. It makes me squirmy and forces me to embrace the grace I thought was reserved for the bad girls. But to my surprise, there's an upside to this good kind of guilt: I have become wowed by God's love for a screwup like me. When I really understand how much God has saved me from, I am able to let go of guilt. My best efforts can't make a dent in my faults, but Jesus' blood is enough to cover them all.

There's a line in TobyMac's peppy song "Love Broke Thru" that makes me weep and fall before God's throne when I hear it: "I was a hopeless fool / Now I'm hopelessly devoted." It's weird for me to identify with a hopeless fool. It's weird to feel the hot tears well up in my eyes while my lips simultaneously curve into a smile. But the depth of my mistakes is a reminder of the depths of God's love for me. The only appropriate response in the face of such radical love is hopeless devotion. Our messes can actually be something to rejoice in because they keep us clinging to him. And that's really where I want to be—right there with him. So if that's what it takes to get me there, I want to embrace this hope-filled feeling of utter dependence on him.

ROCK BOTTOM

On a hot summer day a year ago, I hit rock bottom. From the outside it probably didn't look all that terrible, but in my heart I felt like the worst human being on the planet. I simply couldn't make things right, no matter how hard I tried. I knew the reality of grace by this point, but I still had the subconscious thought that my goodness would be credited to my account. But for that math to make sense, it meant my failings would be deducted from my account as well.

We were in Perdido Key for our annual family beach trip. That meant eight adults plus a two-year-old and a four-month-old were crammed into one condo for seven days. The air was ripe for me to say something dumb, which I did. My sister was the unlikely target. And then, in an effort to take back the dumb thing I said, I heaped on more dumb things. But my words couldn't be taken back. The heaviness of guilt consumed me.

The next morning I woke up early and escaped to the balcony for a few minutes of quiet. This is what I said to God as I watched waves crash against the shore: "I can no longer hide behind good deeds, because in this moment, I feel like I have run out of them. I'm at the bottom—that place where I can't seem to do anything right, and my only option is to grab hold of the life preserver. I've treaded water for too long, depending on my own ability to stay afloat. But now I'm harnessing myself to a better power so I can stop all the doing and rest in your love and grace. Only you can keep me from sinking. Only you can save me from my own requirements for righteousness that I put on myself. I know grace isn't a safety net to fall back on during hard days. It's something I need to live in day to day."

I want to embrace these words of Jesus as my anthem of grace: "Take my yoke upon you, and learn from me, for I am gentle and lowly in heart, and you will find rest for your souls. For my yoke is easy, and my burden is light" (Matthew 11:29-30, ESV). We will all be yoked to something. We can choose the easy and light burden of the Father or the yoke of society and our own guilty thoughts.

I think sometimes we hold on to our guilt because we feel genuinely bad for the pain we've caused. Was my sister still hurt even though I read some nice, comforting things from the Bible? Yes. I couldn't take back the word-vomit that came out, but sitting in my own guilt did a disservice to her as well as to me. In an attempt to make things better, I assumed that exuding untold energy on feeling guilty would help. It didn't. It never does. Guilt just keeps the focus on us and turns the attention to how we are suffering instead of how the other person may be feeling. When we put grace in the space we would normally fill with guilt, true healing can begin.

YOU CAN HAVE MORE THAN ONE ROCK BOTTOM

Last week I was having another one of those days when I felt like I was screwing up everything I attempted to do. I went to bed feeling super discouraged and like a failure. My husband tried to encourage me, but I wasn't having it. For some reason I preferred to have a pity party and imagine that there was no way God could love me.

I woke up the next morning a little more rational, but my heart was still heavy. I have a print of Lamentations 3:22-23 hanging in my bathroom, and it caught my eye. So I dug in to the passage: "The steadfast love of the Lord never ceases; his mercies never come to an end; they are new every morning; great is your faithfulness" (ESV). I'd heard this passage before, but I don't think I'd ever read it while feeling so broken and in such dire need of steadfast love and mercy. When you're in a spot like that, the words take on a whole new meaning. As I read the rest of Lamentations 3 and applied it to my situation, I uncovered these practical steps for when we've hit bottom:

1. **Repent.** According to these verses, the mercies aren't for everyone—they're for those who repent. Repentance isn't simply asking for forgiveness but turning away from the sin. Maybe you really did screw up, but it's not too late to turn around.

2. **Rejoice in a fresh start.** Don't cling to your sin. Suffering in false guilt doesn't make you noble or considerate of others. It's faithless. Lamentations 3:22 in the New International Version says that because of his love "we are not consumed." Yet I sometimes *choose* to be consumed with guilt when God has already set me free with his love. Sometimes we feel like sitting in our guilt gives us a self-imposed time-out. It's paying our dues, right? Nope. We do need to bring a repentant heart to the Lord, but we can't confuse that with self-imposed guilt.

3. **Remember that you can't out-sin God's grace.** The Lord's mercies never end. *The Message* says that his mercies are *created* every morning. I love this visual, because although I know God doesn't ration his grace, I may feel like it goes stale sometimes. This shows that his forgiveness is fresh—he doesn't give it begrudgingly but offers it lavishly, beyond my expectations.

4. **Trust and seek him.** The chapter goes on to give us hope and encouragement, telling us, "The LORD is good to those who wait [confidently] for Him, to those who seek Him [on the authority of God's word]" (verse 25, AMP). We can depend on God, confident that he will meet us as we diligently seek after him.

5. **Don't pick up those burdens again.** God never asked us to keep wallowing in guilt after it's been forgiven.

In fact, he tells us not to: "As far as the east is from the west, so far does he remove our transgressions from us" (Psalm 103:12, ESV). If you have any number of kids, I'm betting you have enough picking up to do. So leave your burdens on the floor, and let our gracious God toss them farther than you could ever imagine.

DID YOU DO ENOUGH?

What about the daily guilt most of us moms feel? I'm not sure where your guilt buttons are, but maybe they look something like this:

- *There wasn't enough time to spend intentional moments with each child.*
- *There wasn't enough time to respond to my friends' texts.*
- *There wasn't enough time to cook a decent meal or wash the dishes.*
- *There wasn't enough time to connect with my husband, let alone sit down and breathe.*
- *There wasn't enough time to pray or crack open my Bible.*

Most nights I have an inner dialogue that I call my "state of the day address." I run through this list of things I should have done that day. (Side note: Isn't that a defeated way to go to sleep? Is it any wonder that up to half of Americans struggle with insomnia?)

Elisabeth Elliot, mild mannered though she might have been, punches me in the gut in the midst of my tortured musings: "There is always enough time to do the will of God. For that we can never say, 'I don't have time.' When we find ourselves frantic and frustrated, harried and harassed and 'hassled,' it is a sign that we are running on our own schedule, not on God's."[2]

She must have gotten a glimpse into my life, because I am frantic many days. I'm trying to run my own schedule instead of letting God lead. Why do I run ahead of God? Because I have things to do, people to see, bills to pay, people to save, countries to feed, hatred to erase. I justify these goals as noble, but inevitably this cycle leads to failure and discouragement.

Day after day, I pick up a yoke that's way heavier than what God intended for me to carry. It's not just that I want to be free from feeling guilty; I want to radically change my life. Can you even fathom a world where moms don't say they're short on time? Can you imagine hearing, "Oh, we're doing great! I did exactly what the Lord had for me today, and I'm more than happy with that!"

It sounds a little nutty, no? That's not because it's impossible but because we've heard a different narrative from the world for too long. The yoke God has for us is freedom from a never-ending list of things we *could* do. Instead, we simply need to focus on doing the will of God. That sounds delightful to me. I can feel the weight coming off my shoulders even now.

I just started reading through the Bible in a year for the first time, which feels very 2007 to me. I might as well tell you I decided to learn how to do the Cupid Shuffle or the Macarena. Though it took me years to finally get brave enough to do this, I'm so glad I did. Here's what I'm realizing as I read the Bible as a full story: God's master plan doesn't hinge on any one of us. He isn't waiting on you to tithe so he can feed the poor. He isn't holding his breath until your next brilliant Instagram post that will encourage moms. (I may be the only narcissist who needs that reminder.) His whole plan won't fall apart if you decide to stop leading that Bible study and take a semester off.

Instead, God *chooses* to use us and longs for us to be a part of his work. Not because all will fail if we don't, but because this is big, exciting Kingdom stuff, and he invites us to be part of what he's doing. Thank the Lord, his criteria for who he uses isn't limited to A-listers and Holy Rollers.

You've likely heard laundry lists of screwups in the Bible whom God used for his purposes, but indulge me while I rehash a few of my favorites. Joseph was the spoiled little brother who didn't mind flaunting it. (I may be able to relate—my family hates playing games with me because I'm the sorest winner of all time. And this wouldn't be a big deal . . . except that I win a lot. Did I just prove their point?) Jacob tricked his twin brother out of his birthright. (I'd *never* do that to my twin sister . . . unless it was a really, really good birthright, like a monthly massage for life.) Moses killed a man and whined about not being a good public speaker. (Um, yep. That's me too. Well, just the public speaking thing. Not the murdering business.) Adam and Eve botched things up right out of the gate by eating the forbidden fruit. (If the forbidden fruit had been chocolate, I obviously would have been in trouble.)

And y'all, this is the legacy of Jesus! None of God's plans were derailed by their mistakes or their slowness to listen. God's plans prevailed because he's God. (And thank the Lord, we're not.)

The fact that God can use mistake-making humans should remind us that our own mistakes don't disqualify us. Those screwups we just mentioned? Joseph saved his family (and ultimately the line of Jesus) from famine. Jacob became a patriarch of the faith. Moses led his people out of slavery in Egypt. Adam and Eve had the distinction of walking with God himself.

Can you imagine if Adam and Eve had thought to themselves, *Each decision we make carries the weight of all humanity*? How paralyzing is that? Instead, our perspective should be that we *get* to be part of God's plan. We *get* to be used by him. We *get* to serve him by serving others.

Let's change the narrative and wave a fond farewell to mommy guilt. No doubt Grumpy Mom will try to come back and remind you of your shortcomings, but keep pummeling the false guilt with reminders of the size of your God. No matter how big of a load you're carrying, he is bigger.

ACTION STEPS

1. **Meditate on the love of God.** When I get an accurate picture of God's love, I find freedom from guilt and end up passing that grace on to my kids, too. Write out any of the burdens that you might be holding on to. Then read Romans 8:38-39 and know that nothing on your list can separate you from God's love. Prayerfully ask God to help you believe that with all your heart.

2. **Ask for forgiveness and do a 180.** Repentance calls us to live differently. When you've been convicted about some sin in your life, don't return to pick it up again, and don't continue to bemoan it. Ask for God's forgiveness and then let it go. If God can release it, we should too.

3. **Pray that your mistakes point your kids to Christ.** Contrary to what we assume, our mistakes don't have to screw up our kids. Instead, our shortcomings can point them to Jesus. Make it your prayer that God would redeem even your worst mistakes in the lives of your kids.

KEY VERSE

Take my yoke upon you, and learn from me, for I am gentle and lowly in heart, and you will find rest for your souls. For my yoke is easy, and my burden is light.

MATTHEW 11:29-30, ESV

PRAYER

Lord, you know that motherhood draws attention to my flaws. Every day I seem to put my foot in my mouth, yell too loudly, forget something important, or do something I regret. Forgive me for my sins, and free me from the guilt I feel when I make mistakes. Remind me that just as my kids are learning and growing, I am too. Thank you for loving me unconditionally. Show me how to rest in that grace. Please help me to give up the burdens I hold on to that you never asked me to carry. Let me find freedom in your love, and let that love spur me on to love you more. In Jesus' name, amen.

PART FOUR

CONNECT

Chapter 13

THE NOT-SO-QUIET TIME

Say Hello to Living in God's Presence

QUIET TIMES, HUH? Does that phrase instantly make you feel guilty, like you don't do enough when it comes to your spiritual life? Do you feel frustrated with your kids, who wake up at the crack of dawn and ruin any plans you might have to spend time with the Lord? Do you feel behind on your day before your feet even hit the ground, and you have no idea how you could squeeze in one more thing to your schedule?

There are two opposing lies about quiet times, and both can drag us down:

1. It's the law.
2. It's optional.

You might be assuming that one of these has to be true, but in reality both are wrong.

Did you know that having an hour-long quiet time in the morning isn't in the Ten Commandments? The Word doesn't tell us there's one right style of Bible study, one specific version of Scripture, or one time of day that's acceptable. And as a further news flash, checking "quiet time" off your list for the day won't get you fast-tracked into heaven or secure a fancier crown for you when you get there.

At the same time, if we desire to live our lives with Jesus, spending time with him isn't optional. It's the way we connect with him, just like we would with anyone else. Every moment of the day, we are in need of him. So to even think we have a choice about spending time with him is silly. The choice is not "Do I need him today?" or "Can I fly solo today?" There's no discussion.

So if both these extremes are off base, we need a third way when it comes to the idea of quiet time. We have to reposition our hearts and remember that our time with the Lord is not intended to fulfill the law. Jesus already did that. Our time with the Lord is a gift so we can know God and be fed and nourished for what we are called to do each day. It's not an obligation to add to our already-full calendars. This is actually what gives us strength as we respond to that calendar, as well as to our kids and our spouse, with joy and patience.

If I don't spend quality time with the Lord, I'm not the mom I want to be. I used to feel bad about this, and I wondered if my quiet time was a crutch. Why did I have to keep coming back to God when I'd spent the last twenty years getting to know him? Couldn't I handle one little morning without him?

Now I know better. I can't.

And I no longer feel bad about that. As soon as I start to think I can handle the world or even the day on my own, I won't survive. Grumpy Mom inevitably comes onto the scene.

This isn't intended to overwhelm you but to empower you as you realize that we were never intended to carry everything on our own. We weren't equipped to do this motherhood thing solo, so fortunately for us, we have ongoing access to the one who is perfectly equipped.

GIVE YOUR TWO COINS

So what does this mean for the mom who barely sleeps and whose kids wake up at five in the morning? I won't insist that you need to get up at 4:30. I am not a monster!

I love the story of the innkeeper in Bethlehem, because I can relate to his situation. He was full. He was maxed out and had no occupancy. Yet I like to think he made room for baby Jesus. It was messy, but he made it happen. You might be in a season where the best you can give is ten minutes, and even that isn't quality, unless you count the *Doc McStuffins* theme song in the background as worship music. There are times when we have to be okay with whatever scraps we have to give to God. God doesn't see them as scraps.

Let's take a look at the story of the widow with two coins:

> Jesus sat down opposite the place where the offerings were put and watched the crowd putting their money into the temple treasury. Many rich people threw in large amounts. But a poor widow came and put in two very small copper coins, worth only a few cents. Calling his disciples to him, Jesus said, 'Truly I tell you, this poor widow has put more into the treasury than all the others. They all gave out of their wealth; but she, out of her poverty, put in everything—all she had to live on.'"
> MARK 12:41-44, NIV

Though you may feel impoverished by your lack of focused time with God, don't discount what you do have to offer. Keep giving it to him with a joyful heart. The Lord is delighted when we give all we have. And I have to believe that our small offering is worth more than a larger offering by those who have all day. The key is adjusting our mind-set and expectations, knowing that this is the season we're in, and then making sure it doesn't become an excuse after the season ends.

WHAT DO WE REALLY HAVE TO OFFER?

All that said, I don't want to let us off the hook too easily. I think we are often convinced that we have only two coins to give, when in reality we have a purse full of dollar bills. The truth is that we feel what time we have to give should be portioned out to other tasks. That's why it's so important for us to reposition the way we think about our time with God. We need to stop seeing it as something we do simply to appease God, like hanging out with that girl just to be nice, not out of an actual desire for friendship. You know what I'm talking about—for some friends you'll fly across the country to hang out with them, and for others you won't even shift your laundry night.

I don't just want to fly across the country to spend time with God; I want to move mountains. I want to make sacrifices, and I want those sacrifices to speak not only to how much I need him but also to how much I genuinely love being with him. I want him to not just fill the little corners of my day but to go everywhere with me. I know he's always with me, but I want to live with an awareness of his presence, even when I'm going grocery shopping or driving to a playdate or eating Chef Vivi's specialty: pretend red onions and bell peppers.

I had one of the most worship-filled experiences of my life

the other day sitting in Vivi's room while she and Vana played in their play kitchen and I folded laundry. I had turned on Kristene DiMarco's "Be Still" and heard these words: "Seasons come and go / But You have never left."

This gave me such a visual of Jesus with me. I vividly pictured him standing in the doorway of Vivi's room and felt such an overwhelming sense of strength and joy. Sometimes being a mom can be lonely, even when we're surrounded by our kids. Your husband may have to work late or your girlfriends may all be busy, but Jesus is always with you. You are never alone.

When we're weary, we need to remember that the time we invest with the Lord gives us life and energy even when we're tired of playing pretend on our kid's bedroom floor.

Over the years I've talked to tons of moms, both in person and through social media, and I've found that those who spend time with God get creative in doing so. Just like that innkeeper. I bet lots of innkeepers in Bethlehem had stables, but he was the one who thought to offer it. Some moms skip Netflix in the evenings and grab their Bibles instead. Some turn their cars into prayer chambers, and others make their kitchens into places of worship. When we get creative, we find him.

And friends, God *longs* to be found. He isn't hiding from us like an enemy; he's like a father playing hide-and-seek with his kids—he sticks out a toe and coughs to draw attention to himself.

Hear me when I say we do need extended time with the Lord—more than shooting up thirty-second prayers or glancing at a verse at a stoplight or the other creative ways we spend time with God. These practices can be really powerful, but only if we have a solid foundation for our relationship. It's hard to start friendships long distance, but if we have a history of connecting on a regular basis, we can pick up where we left off. It's the same with God. If we can create a solid relationship through consistent chunks of time with him, we can keep the conversation going throughout the day.

Spending time with God isn't as *urgent* as the other tasks before us, but here's why it's so important:

- **It's essential to becoming more like him.** Transformation can't happen if we don't give ourselves space to shape our thoughts. Proverbs 4:23 says, "Guard your heart above all else, for it determines the course of your life." Spending adequate time with the Lord is a prime way to guard our hearts.
- **It's essential to our Kingdom work.** Saundra Dalton-Smith says, "We can never reflect the glory of God unless we are gazing in His direction."[1] Time in God's presence gives us the ability to reflect his glory to others. As much as we might convince ourselves that people need us, what they need most is Jesus. Our main role is to be a reflection of him and point others to him.

We have to regularly get away from the noise and create space for God to speak to us. When we do, it's a concrete way of telling God, "I'm ready to listen." If you are feeling frustrated that God seems distant, it may be time to evaluate your commitments and your time with God and decide how to respond.

GOING DARK

When you write a book about doing motherhood differently from the way the world does it, you start noticing how much the Bible has to say on the matter. Ephesians 4:17-24 says,

This I say and testify in the Lord, that you must no
longer walk as the Gentiles do, in the futility of their
minds. They are darkened in their understanding,
alienated from the life of God because of the ignorance
that is in them, due to their hardness of heart. They
have become callous and have given themselves up to
sensuality, greedy to practice every kind of impurity.
But that is not the way you learned Christ!—assuming
that you have heard about him and were taught in him,
as the truth is in Jesus, to put off your old self, which
belongs to your former manner of life and is corrupt
through deceitful desires, and to be renewed in the
spirit of your minds, and to put on the new self, created
after the likeness of God in true righteousness and
holiness (ESV).

A few things stick out to me about the people Paul is describing in this passage:

1. Their understanding is darkened.
2. They are alienated from God.
3. Their hearts are hardened.

Does this describe us some days? It sure sounds like me at
times. And this is supposed to be a description of the unbelieving Gentile, not the way of the believer.

We need to be careful not to walk in the "futility of [our]
minds." This kind of faulty thinking usually happens when
our communication with God starts to taper off. The distance
between us and God creeps in gradually. We sacrifice our time
with God at the hands of being responsible for keeping a few
little humans alive. This is worthwhile stuff, but at some point

it becomes an excuse for letting our souls get depleted, and before we know it our hearts become callous and unfeeling.

When we keep choosing to come back to God, however, our focus muscles build. We're able to pray in the midst of distractions and not feel like we need absolute silence. This is pretty much a necessity if you have a kid, right?

Getting alone with God might look like fifteen minutes in the stillest part of your day to sit and study the Word so you can learn more about who God is. It might look like lying on the floor with hands open, asking God to fill you up and use you for his Kingdom that day. We can't spend time with the creator of the universe and not be changed.

It can be challenging to consistently spend time with God, but the good news is that the more we do it, the more momentum we gain and the easier it is to keep going. Darren Hardy describes the process of developing any habit in *The Compound Effect*: "It's like the wheels of a steam locomotive. At a standstill, it takes very little to keep it from moving forward—a one-inch block of wood placed under the front wheel will do the job. . . . But once the train starts rolling, the wheels get into a rhythm. If the pressure remains consistent, the train gains momentum, and watch out! At 55 miles an hour, that train can crash through a five-foot, steel-reinforced concrete wall and keep on going."[2] We can be stopped by a little piece of wood, or we can plow through steel and concrete. We can get distracted by a fly buzzing around our bedroom or dishes in the sink, or we can pray through moments of fear while *Tangled* is playing in the background or while we are staring at a full in-box.

E. M. Bounds says, "Satan wants us to let the grass grow on the path to our prayer chamber."[3] The devil whispers excuses to us like "You can skip time with God just this once" or "You don't have time for that today" because he knows what happens when we stop connecting with God. He knows that distance will leave us weary, impatient, and grumpy. But we're not going to let him win. Not today, Satan.

LOOK OUT, BIBLE STUDY GIRLS

If you are a good quiet-time-in-the-morning gal like me, you may be thinking you'll escape this chapter unscathed. Brace yourself.

Your morning quiet time isn't cutting it.

I used to think that my morning time with the Lord was like a big, hearty breakfast that would get me through the day. It turns out, I was wrong. I was demanding that a chunk of time in the morning with God would carry me through the next twenty-four hours. Sure, I'd pray or read some verses throughout the day if I had time, but I saw that as a bonus.

I found myself frustrated that I could have amazing quiet times and be filled with the Spirit, and then a few hours later, I'd forget about him and lose all that joy and peace. I could tell the Lord I was ready to surrender the day to him, and within a span of ten minutes, I'd be yelling at my kids.

Here's the thing: ongoing time with the Lord isn't about marking another thing off our to-do lists. It's about being so awake to his love and grace that our only response is to want more of him. It's about coming to the Father with the expectation that more time with him will change us. It's about realizing that he's already with us; we simply need to look for him and stop looking to the worthless things around us for fulfillment.

I don't want to be satisfied with mere crumbs. I want to feast throughout the day in the presence of God.

ACTION STEPS

1. **Keep a Bible open on your counter.** Just the sight of God's Word focuses my heart on him. And reading even a few verses throughout the day keeps his Word on my lips.

2. **Spend the first few minutes of your kids' nap time in prayer or in the Word.** I used to think I couldn't do this because I needed every second of nap time for work. What I found was that I normally wasted ten to fifteen minutes anyway. Now, with the motivation of spending time with the Lord, I stay focused and get right down to work afterward.

3. **Use your phone to point you to prayer or Scripture.** You can use a daily reminder or a Bible app notification to prompt you to spend time with the Lord. You might even make it your routine to always hop on the Bible app before going on social media.

4. **Let your kids sit next to you while you spend time with the Lord.** Once I realized the blessing of having my kids see me spend time with Jesus and not just hear me talk about it, I've learned to enjoy the times when one of them wakes up early. What a precious memory for our kids to see their mom devouring the Word!

KEY VERSE

I will meditate on your precepts and fix my eyes on your ways. I will delight in your statutes; I will not forget your word.

PSALM 119:15-16, ESV

PRAYER

*Father, I need you every moment of the day.
Remind me that the foundation of my days with
you is knowing who you are through prayer and
your Word. Help me to reject the lie that I don't
have time for you. Give me creativity and flexibility to embrace time with you in unique ways based
on this particular season. Put a hunger for your
Word in me, and keep distractions at bay so I can
dig in and understand what you are saying to me.
In Jesus' name, amen.*

Chapter 14

ROLE CALL

Say Hello to a Thriving Marriage

WOULDN'T IT BE SO MUCH EASIER if marriage and mother-hood were independent of each other? Maybe we could spend the first half of our lives married and really get to enjoy those years to the fullest. We could take trips, go on romantic dates, and engage in deep conversations, and then we could part ways and spend the next half of life investing in motherhood, nur-turing little hearts, reading books to our kids, and being the room mom.

That sounds ridiculous, no? When we try to picture these relationships separately, it's clear that marriage is a foundation for parenting. But it's easy to fall into the world's lie that kids have to be the priority and marriage must take a backseat once kids show up.

I won't pretend that kids don't throw a kink into marriage, but if we accept the world's view, we forfeit a strong foundation for the very kids we're giving everything up for. This is typically when Grumpy Mom unpacks her bags and decides to stay awhile.

RATIONS OF GRACE

On a few occasions, after getting into an argument with my husband, I used to go into my daughter's room and cuddle with her if Tyler and I couldn't resolve our conflict right away. I longed for immediate connection and acceptance, so instead of choosing humility and mending things with my husband, I chose stubbornness and escaped to a toddler bed that was warm and cozy and home to a little girl who was eager to have Mommy's unexpected cuddles. I hated that I did this. It felt like I was using my daughter, and at the same time, I was making my husband feel like I was fine without him.

The thing is, our kids are often easier to forgive than our husband. We can chalk up their dumb behavior to not knowing better or, hey, being a three-year-old. But what's our husband's excuse? We hold our husband to a higher standard (which isn't completely ludicrous), but this shows a misunderstanding of grace on our part.

We think someone should get more grace if they deserve it. If they should know better, they should get less grace. But this is anything but grace. What if we could forgive the offenses of our spouse just as quickly as we forgive the offenses of our kids? Grace, by its very definition, is not given to those who are worthy of it.

Hebrews 12:14-15 says, "Make every effort to live in peace with everyone and to be holy; without holiness no one will see the Lord. See to it that no one falls short of the grace of God and that no bitter root grows up to cause trouble and defile many" (NIV). This isn't a passage you normally hear at weddings, but it is packed with wisdom for marriage. When we live at peace with our spouse, it glorifies God. People who are on the outside looking in will see the Lord's character when we choose forgiveness, grace, and peace.

The Message's paraphrase of this passage includes a few phrases I love:

- "Make sure no one gets left out of God's generosity." Grace flows from God's generosity, not mine. It's not for me to choose who to dole out his generosity to. This awareness challenges me to stop analyzing who deserves something that isn't even mine to give.
- "Keep a sharp eye out for weeds of bitter discontent." We need to be as vigilant about recognizing bitterness as we are about the more obvious areas that need our attention. How many times will we watch like a hawk what our children eat, how they play on the playground, or what shows they see, and then neglect this heart issue with our spouse? Bitterness may pop up, but if we are keeping a sharp eye out for it, we can stop it from taking root.
- "A thistle or two gone to seed can ruin a whole garden in no time." Holding on to hurts doesn't just ruin us. It has the potential to ruin the whole family. What starts out as a tiny thistle of a complaint gets planted, and then it's fed by our negative thoughts about our spouse or by a comparison to our friend's husband—or perhaps by a stubborn escape to our daughter's room.

LOUD NOISES AND EXTRA HANDS

One of the reasons we prioritize our children over our spouse is because our kids' needs are usually more obvious. My husband can make himself dinner. He can dress himself and even turn on the TV by himself. If we feel like we're in survival mode, our instinct is to respond to the loudest noise. Our days are often determined by which fires need to be put out instead of by our priorities.

My husband rarely has the loudest need in our home. Because of that, I have to be really intentional about hearing him. I have to be diligent in asking how I can serve him. If I don't, I forget that he has any needs of his own and simply see him as a workhorse.

In her book *Lists to Love By for Busy Wives*, Susan Merrill says, "I thought of [my husband] as an extension of myself, two more hands to keep our family of seven operable."[1] I can't tell you how this quote has had me thinking over the last few weeks. This is me. When my husband comes home, I think of all the things he can help me do. He can bathe our youngest while I tidy up. He can take the girls for a walk while I take a few minutes to myself. After a long day, this is naturally where my mind flows. This is simply what being in a partnership and raising a family together is about, right? It's true that this is part of the marriage relationship, but if this is our sole focus, our souls will wither and we'll become the mom with the butler husband who uses her kids as her security blanket. Or the husband and wife who have to awkwardly rediscover life as a couple when their kids leave the nest.

Depth in motherhood requires depth in marriage. So where can we start? How do we stop seeing our spouse as another set of hands to help tackle our to-do lists? (Scratch that. It's normally *my* list.)

Let's start with this classic example.

The day-to-day responsibilities of motherhood often have me wishing I could sit quietly and not talk for a while. I'm weary from telling my kids to get that electrical plug away from their mouths, to stop standing on the chair, to be nice to their sister. I get tired of hearing my own voice. I long for moments when I can clock out from the command center. By the time late afternoon hits, the witching hour has begun. I'm mentally ready for bedtime, but I'd just be satisfied with seeing my husband walk through the door. I have a load to dump on him. It comes in the form of chores, a recap of the roughest parts of my day, and sometimes literally my kids.

By the time Tyler gets home, I've spent the last nine hours barking orders. By that point, though, I'm on a roll. Is it any wonder that wives are stereotyped as nags who constantly tell their husbands what to do? We are expected to keep order from sunrise to sunset, and then we're supposed to instantly turn it off when our husband walks through the door?

I remember my mom telling me that this desire wives have to control their husbands is actually biblical. Not good biblical, but based-in-truth biblical. She pointed me to Genesis 3:16: "[God] said to the woman, 'I will sharpen the pain of your pregnancy, and in pain you will give birth. And you will desire to control your husband, but he will rule over you.'" This tension we feel in marriage is part of the curse. We will long for control over our husband against God's design.

And then I'm reminded that my husband is not off the hook when it comes to the curse either. In Genesis 3:17, God says to Adam, "Since you listened to your wife and ate from the tree whose fruit I commanded you not to eat, the ground is cursed because of you. All your life you will struggle to scratch a living from it." Doesn't this describe a common struggle men experience—feeling overwhelmed with the responsibility to provide for their families? As I consider these struggles from the curse, I see how they play a role in our everyday lives. Your family might not have the same roles, but I think this biblical truth represents something that goes beyond each family's unique circumstances.

I've heard it said plenty of times that husbands should use the drive home to switch gears from their work stresses so they can be present and enjoy their families. (And when I say I've heard this, I mainly mean I've suggested it to my husband.) But now I'm starting to see that wives need to do the same thing. How can our husband's arrival home act as a trigger for us to switch gears from instructor to loving wife? And how can we do this without ditching the kids for an hour-long massage first?

A BREAKDOWN OF COMMUNICATION

My husband and I have an ongoing joke that he can spend all day with his friend for a fishing trip and within the first five minutes of his arrival home, we will have already spoken more words to each other than he and his friend did all day.

We women love to talk.

And the natural progression in a lot of relationships is that husbands start to tune out. There are just too many words for them to possibly hear them all. I get that there's science to back up why we talk more than men do, so we kind of have a valid reason for all the words, but we can't use that as an excuse for poor communication in our marriage. The Bible offers wisdom about how we can find peace and joy in our relationships, even when there's a mismatch in communication styles.

Let's take a look at a big, scary passage about submission that makes me want to yell, "Look over there!" and slither out of the room. But today there will be no army crawls across the floor—we're going to tackle it head-on.

In the same way, you wives, be submissive to your own husbands [subordinate, not as inferior, but out of respect for the responsibilities entrusted to husbands and their accountability to God, and so partnering with them] so that even if some do not obey the word [of God], they may be won over [to Christ] without discussion by the godly lives of their wives, when they see your modest and respectful behavior [together with your devotion and appreciation—love your husband, encourage him, and enjoy him as a blessing from God.]
1 PETER 3:1-2, AMP

There's a lot packed into these verses, so let's break it down a bit.

- "Not as inferior, but out of respect for the responsibilities entrusted to husbands and their accountability to God." God has entrusted some things to your husband, not you. Ouch. This passage doesn't explicitly list all those things. Wouldn't that have been nice? "Husbands, you are entrusted with earning the main source of income, managing retirement plans, and taking out the trash." It's not so cut and dried, which requires us to stay in tune with the Holy Spirit. But just knowing that there are things God gave to my husband and not to me reminds me that I don't need to try to take over everything. It also encourages me to ask God what things he has given to my husband so I'm able to support him well in those areas.
- "Won over . . . without discussion." So this is really possible? Most of the time I assume our conflicts need all my words, but this passage indicates that's not the case. Although this passage is referring to unbelieving

husbands being won over in faith, I think it holds true in other areas too. I tend to think it's my job to steer my husband like a stubborn ox back onto the path. That leads to a relentless and overbearing Valerie, and I'll tell you what, she doesn't win anyone over.

- "Modest." The way we follow Christ speaks volumes. The goal here is humility. That doesn't necessarily mean silence, but it leaves room for my husband to hear Christ instead of just me. When we stop talking so much, we give our spouse the opportunity to hear what God is saying to them instead of creating a twelve-point defense for the case we're bringing against them.

- "Respectful behavior." We can show respect to our husbands by acknowledging the incredible role God has given them. Do we appreciate what a heavy weight God has put on a man's shoulders to take care of his family? Or do we see our husbands as sideshows who show up right before bedtime, after we've done all the heavy lifting?

- "Together with your devotion and appreciation." We are to love, encourage, and enjoy our husbands. We should be enthusiastic about their accomplishments and appreciate the work they do. We need to stop seeing them as two extra hands to make our agendas happen. I'm speaking from experience here—I've done this more times than I can count. When we see our husbands as the amazing humans they are, respect and fun come more naturally.

A BIRD'S-EYE VIEW

So we might realize that we need to be intentional about building a strong marriage, but how do we do that, practically speaking? There are plenty of ways to work on your marriage—reading books, attending conferences, scheduling date nights—but for me the thing that has been most pivotal in creating a healthy marriage has been to get a mentor.

My mentor helps me see the big picture when it comes to my relationship with Tyler. Mrs. Carol is a wise woman at my church who has graciously taken me under her wing. We meet once a month with the primary purpose of helping me grow. She encourages me in many ways, but one of the most frequent reminders she gives me is to pull back, get an aerial view of my life (specifically my marriage), and see how the thing that frustrates me actually fits in to the larger perspective.

On a recent visit with Mrs. Carol, I had spent twenty minutes unloading my latest grievances about my husband and feeling the weight of all this when she gave me a much-needed reality check. We were sitting on my porch, which is possibly my favorite "room" in our house, and she simply asked me to take an inventory of my life as it really is. She knew a good bit about Tyler and his character already, and she knew that the issues I was bringing up weren't as significant as I thought they were in the moment. She told me to step back and get a big-picture view of my life. I started making a mental list, and I was overwhelmed in the best possible way. In just a few moments, I was reminded how truly blessed my life is.

When I look at the full picture, I see so much goodness. I see how our family is growing. I see the good decisions we're making. I become instantly grateful for my husband and my life. This is not my default setting. During those seasons when there are no big fires to put out, I find myself in the weeds, analyzing every leaf for possible complaints. And when you're looking that closely, you'll inevitably find something.

We have to decide to be content and not place the same weight on the small things that we do on the big things. It's true that there are some deep wounds that come in the context of marriage, and I don't want to minimize those in any way. But we need to be careful to ensure that our emotional, mental, and physical responses match the size of the issue. It's time to stop majoring on the minors in our lives and marriages, in conversations with both our spouse and our friends. Let's step back and see the big picture and address big things with seriousness and small things with less intensity.

It turns out that Grumpy Wife is closely related to Grumpy Mom, so if we can send one packing, the other is sure to follow.

ACTION STEPS

1. **Pray more than you criticize.** Our energy is much better spent bringing our criticisms to the God of the universe first rather than dumping them prematurely on our husband. Prayer gives us an opportunity to turn a bitter heart that might be looking for a fight into a heart that's more aligned with the Lord's.

2. **Humanize your husband.** Return your husband's brain, legs, and hands to him. Remember that God has entrusted some responsibilities just to him.

3. **Prioritize laughter.** Laughing with your husband is often more productive than getting ahead on the laundry or making sure there are no dishes in the sink. This is something I have to work on. While laughing with my husband might not seem efficient, it sets the tone in our house, refuels our weary bones, and creates intimacy. When we laugh together, Grumpy Mom takes a holiday—and she takes her husband with her.

KEY VERSE

See to it that no one falls short of the grace of God and that no bitter root grows up to cause trouble and defile many.

HEBREWS 12:15, NIV

PRAYER

Father, forgive me for viewing marriage as if my husband and I are two cocaptains trying to manage a team. Shift my heart, and put a desire in me to be intentional about my marriage. Remind me that the time I invest in my marriage is also an investment in my kids as they see a godly marriage lived out. Fill our home with love and respect, laughter and joy. In Jesus' name, amen.

Chapter 15

PLAYS WELL WITH OTHERS

Say Hello to Real Friendship

YEARS AGO, WHEN TYLER AND I were newly married, we talked about how our parents didn't really have friends. It wasn't because they were losers. In fact, we consider ourselves really blessed to have sane, even fun, parents. We knew it wasn't them. So we chalked it up to the fact that while they were raising us, they must not have had time to make friends. Now it's funny to see them thriving and having better plans for New Year's Eve or the weekend than Tyler and I do.

In some ways, this ebb and flow is a natural part of life. Some seasons are simply more conducive to friendships than others. But although the amount and type of contact might change, God's design for community is not a seasonal thing. It's a thread that runs throughout our entire lives. We were created for community.

I have a hunch we've all said something to this effect at some point: *I don't have time for friendships in this season. I'm just too busy with my kids.*

The problem with this line of reasoning is that it has been uttered by moms in every season—moms of newborns, moms of toddlers, working moms, homeschooling moms, moms of kids just starting school, moms of teenagers, and even moms of new moms. So essentially, if we bought into this lie, we wouldn't have time for friendship in any season.

I'll be totally honest and tell you this is one chapter I wish someone else could have written for me. I don't have this figured out yet, so I'm going to do my best to stumble my way through. I have a feeling I'm going to step on my own toes here, but I can't write this book about lies that get smuggled into our hearts without mentioning this one.

I want to believe God's truth about friendship and unity with other believers. Scripture calls us to "encourage one another" (Hebrews 10:25) and to be "devoted to one another in love" (Romans 12:10, NIV).

I don't want to be the woman who, when life gets busy, lets her time with friends be the first thing to go and neglects this portion of the Word for the sake of convenience. Though friendship might look different during busy seasons of motherhood, that doesn't change the fact that God still calls us to real, meaningful relationships.

So together, let's figure out what friendship looks like when our hands and our calendars are full. If we can get this right, it won't be just one more item for our to-do list; it will be something that brings soul-level refreshment.

WHAT DO YOU EXPECT?

I have a confession to make. When it comes to friendship, I'm just plain lazy. I don't want to put the work in, but I still very much desire those deep conversations and belly laughs. I long for the spiritual encouragement and the prayers. And just as much, I long to be there for someone else in the same ways.

Besides the laziness that holds me back, I'm also an ROI girl. I want a high return on my investment. And truth be told, those dreaded, awkward conversations at the beginning stages of a friendship don't feel worth the time. Case in point: the girls' night where you don't know many people and you put yourself out there, but it ends up being uncomfortable and in no way resembling the intimacy you're longing for.

We have plenty of excuses for not making time with friends, and many of these are related to other lies we believe about motherhood:

- *We're always tired.* Small talk can drain us if we're already weary.
- *We can't take time for ourselves.* We assume our kids simply couldn't manage without us.
- *We're victims of busyness.* We think our schedules won't allow time for friends.

We let these lies convince us that the work it takes to develop deep friendships isn't worth it. And this is where we start missing out on good things God intended for us.

WE MISS THE BLESSING

Sometimes we miss out on the community that's right in front of us because we have an idealized version of what friendship should look like. You know, the kind of relationship where you can walk into each other's houses without knocking, sit and talk for hours, or take trips together. In this stage of your life, friendship might look more like chaotic Friday lunches at

Chick-fil-A or hanging out in the carpool line, but that's okay. Rejecting friendship just because it isn't perfect would be like a starving person pushing away a sandwich just because it isn't a steak.

We often take it for granted that there are opportunities for friendship all around us—including relationships with other believers. I live in South Louisiana, which is on the edge of the Bible Belt. You can't get a cup of coffee without seeing someone reading their Bible or watching two friends meet up for prayer or Bible study. As a result, I've often taken Christian community for granted. Then I read Dietrich Bonhoeffer's book *Life Together* (a fact my mom would be really proud of, seeing as she talked about Bonhoeffer on an almost weekly basis when I was growing up). He says, "It is by the grace of God that a congregation is permitted to gather visibly in this world to share God's Word and sacrament. Not all Christians receive this blessing."[1]

Bonhoeffer goes on to challenge our ideals about what friendship should look like: "He who loves his dream of a community more than the Christian community itself becomes a destroyer of the latter, even though his personal intentions may be ever so honest and earnest and sacrificial."[2] Ouch! This is me. Our expectations of Christian friendship can end up destroying the very community we're longing for. We have this ideal of what friendship should look like, and when it doesn't happen, we opt out altogether. We opt out because life is hard in this moment. We opt out because playdates are spent wrestling kids instead of having deep, uninterrupted conversations. We opt out because our homes aren't worthy of guests. We opt out because the other person is too different from us.

But opting out means we lose before we even try.

Proverbs 27:17 says, "As iron sharpens iron, so one person sharpens another" (NIV). In theory, most of us want to be refined to look more like Jesus. But we don't go about this refining process in the best way. I choose growing my business over people. I choose reading books over people. I choose hiding my mess over people. I choose soft things to shape me, when the Word says that it's people who will sharpen us. Those other things have their place, but when we isolate ourselves, we're missing out on the biggest tool he uses to shape us. And how cool that this sharpening comes with dinners around the table and funny GIFs texted to us on a hard day!

EMBRACING SISTERHOOD

Being in the thick of motherhood shouldn't sideline us from friendship; instead, it should serve as a reminder of how much we need community. In this season when it's so easy to flip a switch and become Grumpy Mom, doesn't it make sense that we need to be refined by other believers who can challenge our thinking and pull us out of the pit of lies we face? Doesn't it make sense that we'd need someone to share a laugh with when things don't go as planned instead of someone to sulk with? No, it won't happen overnight. And no, it won't be easy. But it will be worth it.

Bonhoeffer was right to challenge us to embrace what Christian brotherhood (and sisterhood) can look like right this minute instead of waiting for what we hope it could be. He isn't saying we shouldn't dream. He's saying we shouldn't miss out on our present blessings while pining for something that doesn't exist. He says, "The physical presence of other Christians is a source of incomparable joy and strength to the believer."[3]

Besides refining us, Christian friendship brings "incomparable joy." Don't we grumpy moms desperately need this? Psalm 133:1 says, "How good and pleasant it is when God's people live together in unity!" (NIV). We are all looking for a little dose of "good and pleasant" in our lives. The question is, how do we get there? I'm guessing you don't have a lot of tranquil coffee shop conversations with jazz music playing in the background. Instead, your conversations are probably taking place to the sound track of kids losing their minds (and shoes) in the Chick-fil-A playground.

The good news is that the foundation for friendship doesn't have to be hours of peaceful, uninterrupted time. Friendship can flourish anywhere as long as we have the one necessary ingredient: love.

Don't stop me if you've heard this one before: "For God so loved the world that he gave his one and only Son, that whoever believes in him shall not perish but have eternal life" (John 3:16, NIV). Okay, so this is just the most famous verse in the Bible, but after I've heard it so many times, the first part is sticking out to me in a new way. God loved the *world*. Not just the Jews. Not just the ones who looked like his Son. Not just the ones who were super kind or obviously talented. He loved everyone.

I wish I had a blanket love like this for people. We know God's love is personal, but I forget that his love is global, too. I wish my instinct were to think the best of every person I meet instead of think the worst until they change my mind. What if we let this radical love of God shift the way we love? His Holy Spirit lives in us, so we have the ability to do this.

You've probably heard before that love is a choice, but what if we started approaching every potential relationship with this thought in mind? What if we chose love without waiting to see how the other person will behave first and then determining the level of love they'll get?

I don't want to be the friend people say things like this about: "I'm just glad she's on my side" or "Just stay on her good side and you'll be okay." These are phrases I've heard in dozens of conversations, between the *Housewives* and my own front porch. I want my default to be love, and I don't want my love to be up for negotiation based on the other person's behavior.

What if we could see people through the eyes of Jesus instead of through the lens of our own preferences?

Where we see differences as flaws and failings as deal breakers, God sees the blood of Jesus. When we recognize that we are all made in the image of God, we are free to be friends with an infinite variety of people.

"JUST BEING HONEST" AND OTHER MISCONCEPTIONS

The world would have us believe that moms spend playdates gossiping about the friend who's not there, judging the mom they won't let in the group, and calling each other out in a passive-aggressive way. We all know how hard it is to prioritize friendships—why would we go to all the effort for something as toxic as this?

A lot could be said about how to create a healthy friendship, but here are the basics:

1. **Don't gossip.** Gossip is not a conversation but a propeller for ungodliness. In 2 Timothy 2:16, Paul says, "Avoid irreverent babble, for it will lead people into more and more ungodliness" (ESV). I have never, not even once, seen gossip move people into godliness.

Though it may seem like it's just words that don't affect anyone else, we fail to recognize what these words do to our hearts. Gossip impacts the way we see someone, the way we judge them, and the way we harbor resentment and unforgiveness.

2. **Don't compare.** When we see amazing qualities in women around us, we are often tempted to envy them and feel bad about ourselves. But instead of comparing, what if we saw how these qualities originated in Jesus first? When we see that mom who seems so calm and gentle with her kids or that friend who finds so much wisdom in the Word or that prayer warrior who finds so much time to pray, what if we channeled every bit of comparison into wanting to be more like Jesus instead? In her book *The Happiness Dare*, Jennifer Dukes Lee says, "If I am trying to be like someone else, it had better be Jesus."[4] Why would we imitate an imitation when we have direct access to Jesus himself? I'm not saying that being influenced by others doesn't have its place, but when it morphs into comparison, I want to let this truth pull me out of a dangerous spiral.

3. **Don't judge.** A judgmental attitude might be the biggest barrier for friendship. Colossians 3:12-13 says, "As God's chosen people, holy and dearly loved, clothe yourselves with compassion, kindness, humility, gentleness and patience. Bear with each other and forgive one another if any of you has a grievance against someone. Forgive as the Lord forgave you" (NIV). I want my default response to be one of compassion and kindness instead of judgment. This would change the disposition of my heart from angst to rest.

4. **Lift each other up.** In the book of Acts, Barnabas was the guy who interceded on behalf of Paul (a former Christian killer, mind you) when the apostles were too afraid to let him join them (see Acts 9). They welcomed Paul because of Barnabas's integrity. Barnabas's name means "encourager," and his life showed this trait even more. Paul was one of the most influential people in the history of Christianity. Meanwhile, sweet Barnabas stood just off to the side of the stage, faithfully serving but gaining nowhere near the same recognition that Paul received. Are we willing to be silent backers? Are we willing to be the backstage help instead of the stars of the show? I hope it can be said of me one day that I was a Barnabas for my friends.

5. **Lift each other out.** True friendship means telling the truth to our friends, even when it's difficult. Ephesians 4:15 says, "We will speak the truth in love, growing in every way more and more like Christ, who is the head of his body, the church." Truth *in love* is the key here. With my judgmental tendencies, I normally err on the side of not giving any type of criticism to other people. (Unless you're my sister. Then you may get the full wrath of my critiques.) It's a risk to hold each other accountable, but this is something God designed as a critical part of friendship. Before we run away with the idea that we just have to be "real" with people, however, we need to make sure we're speaking truth with the right motivation and the right heart. Elisabeth Elliot says, "There is a common belief that a frank expression of what one naturally feels and thinks is always a good thing because it is 'honest.' This is not true. If the feelings and thoughts are wrong in

themselves, how can expressing them verbally add up to something good? It seems to me they add up to three sins: wrong feeling, wrong thought, wrong action."[5] If we can approach conversations with this filter of not just being honest but communicating what is true as well, we will avoid unnecessary pain and actually build trust in our relationships.

The potential for friendship in motherhood is powerful. We can go beyond settling for surface-level conversations and comparing our kids' eating habits and sleeping patterns. It may be uncomfortable to connect on a heart level at first, but if we invest in friendships, they will result in incredible strength and soul-deep connections. As Ecclesiastes 4:9 says, two are better than one—and two are more effective at sending Grumpy Mom packing.

ACTION STEPS

1. **Discover your friends' personalities.** Personality tests have been a really practical way for me to appreciate my friends' differences. My husband took a test that revealed he had "low observational skills." I could have told him that for free! But after years of frustration and wishing he were more detailed or at the very least that he'd notice the half stick of butter that got left out, I'm finding freedom to love that dairy waster without constantly trying to fix him. The same principle applies in my friendships as well.

2. **Make a list of qualities you want in a friend, and then be that friend.** We often complain that it's hard to find good

friends, but how often do we look in the mirror to see if we're good friends ourselves? Luke 6:31 says that we're to "treat others the same way you want them to treat you" (NASB). This Golden Rule pretty much sums up what it means to be a good friend.

3. **Own your choices.** I've heard it said that we have to stop saying, "I can't do _____" and instead say, "This is not a priority." If something is, in fact, a priority, we will make time for it. If you can't eat breakfast, it's likely not a high priority to eat breakfast. This girl doesn't skip a meal. I prioritize breakfast—it doesn't just get skipped. Why? Because I will sacrifice sleep and a few extra dollars, or even eat an old, slimy banana, before I'll skip the meal altogether. Similarly, if I say I don't have time for friendship, what I'm really saying is that it's not a high priority.

KEY VERSE

Treat others the same way you want them to treat you.

LUKE 6:31, AMP

PRAYER

Father, I have believed the lie that friendships during this busy season are nonessential. I know that you created me for community, so please show me how friendships fit into my life. Help me to be the kind of friend I long to have myself. Put the right people in my path, and give me the courage to embrace awkward beginnings, knowing they can blossom into lifelong friendships. In Jesus' name, amen.

Chapter 16

AN OPEN LETTER AGAINST OPEN LETTERS

Say Hello to Relationships without Resentment

OVER THE YEARS, I've noticed the strangest trend gaining momentum: the open letter.

This is not something new, but with the anonymity of the online world, people seem to be braver about putting their opinions out there. Although this phenomenon seems relatively harmless, it can fuel a lot of offended feelings. The anatomy of an open letter goes like this:

1. I'm offended.
2. I don't want to be offended.
3. Here is my way of telling everyone I know about how I'm offended so they won't offend me too or, at the very least, so they'll avoid putting me in an awkward conversation.

Here's the assumption that lurks behind this line of thinking: *No one should ever say anything that offends me.*

Our reputation as moms is that we are some of the greatest offenders and that we're constantly offended.

Here are a few headlines for posts I've seen recently:

- 10 Things You Shouldn't Say to a New Mom
- 13 Things Non-Parents Shouldn't Say to Parents (this one was on a parenting blog, no less!)
- No Mom of Boys Wants to Hear This
- 3 Things to Never Say to a Mom Who Isn't Sleeping
- What You Shouldn't Say to Moms with Four or More Kids

The world wants to convince us that the solution to not being offended is to keep everyone else in line. But we can't control every human on the planet, no matter how viral our letters become. The good news is that God has a better way.

In my own life, I've seen just how grumpy I can become when I take offense. When I hear something that rubs me the wrong way, I have a choice to make. Does this offend me or not? In the past, I'd give this a lot of attention so I could make an educated decision (I'm thorough like that). I'd weigh all the evidence—tone, word choice, political correctness, what was said, what wasn't said—and pick that convo apart. Inevitably I'd decide that I had a right to be offended. Because if you dig deep enough, you're sure to hit something.

Then here's where the spiral would head: I'd take on the role of a victim and drift into feeling sorry for myself. I'd turn inward and feel self-righteous and proud, deciding that I didn't deserve such treatment and that my offender was a monster. And then this internal conversation dumped all over the people in my life (including my two lovely girls). Even the most innocent bystanders weren't safe.

In one particular instance (okay, more than that), I was on my phone and saw a comment on my post that might as well have read, "Valerie, I think what you're doing is dumb and wrong." Almost immediately, I turned on my kids as if they were the ones who had offended me. What's crazy is that the person who hurt me may never even know how she made me feel.

John Bevere has a whole book on taking offense called *The Bait of Satan*. How's that for succinctly calling it like it is? Bevere says, "If we do not deal with an offense, it will produce more fruit of sin, such as bitterness, anger, and resentment."[1] Sounds like a seasoned Grumpy Mom, no? Every time we take offense at something, the devil uses it to his advantage. Our stomachs knot up and we take on a short tone with our kids. Fortunately, though, the Bible is timeless, which means there must have been a fair share of offenders in Paul's day too.

THE NEW LAW

I think open letters (or the times we get together with friends to list our grievances) are the modern-day version of the "foolish discussions" that Titus 3:9 speaks of: "Do not get involved in foolish discussions about spiritual pedigrees or in quarrels and fights about obedience to Jewish laws. These things are useless and a waste of time." We come up with our own code of what's acceptable and what's not. And then if anyone violates what we have deemed the law, we feel like we have permission to be offended.

Our offenses polarize people just as much as political differences do. How is the conversation of whether you breastfeed or not so charged these days? I think it's because each time we get offended, we run even further in the opposite direction. If you read something and agree, you leave a comment saying, "Yeah! Breastfeeding mommas have NOOO idea what it's like," while someone else sees the extreme response and says, "This is ridiculous. ALL non-nursing moms are the worst." These extremes leave no room for grace and just make us think badly of the group we aren't a part of.

The new law we've created with all our "You should . . ." and "I'm offended when . . ." statements doesn't leave room for genuine conversation, let alone friendship, with anyone who disagrees with us. And the silliest part of all is that Jesus came to fulfill the actual law. I know—this might seem like a major jump, but stay with me. The law we put in place and follow religiously like the Pharisees is actually a hologram. It may look real, but it's not. The way we find freedom is by remembering that Jesus fulfilled the law we were never capable of fulfilling ourselves (see Romans 8:1-4).

THE MOTHER OF ALL DAYS

Mother's Day is ripe for offense in our day. What was once a holiday to simply celebrate our moms is now practically a battlefield, and any Mother's Day message must include a long list of caveats. A note to the ones who wish they were moms. A note to the ones who have lost moms. A note to the ones who are currently on bad terms with their moms. A note to single dads. Every year I awkwardly try to make a post that simply thanks my mom and mentions something about my own experience of motherhood. I inevitably get worried someone will find it offensive because I neglected to include all the appendixes.

One particular year, someone shared that she was offended that her friends assumed it was her first Mother's Day because she had just had her first daughter. She said she became a mom during her first pregnancy, in which she eventually lost the baby. Here is the ironic part: I was offended by her offense. I was offended that this simple day of celebration for a mom's hard work (who am I kidding—*my* hard work) was being over-shadowed by someone who was trying to make a statement by rejecting the well-meaning good wishes of others.

Yes, I *wanted* to recognize the loss and hardships some women were experiencing. Yes, I *wanted* to be sympathetic. But instead, I was completely consumed by my feelings of offense. I took it personally, as if this person were directly critiquing my rather straightforward approach to Mother's Day. I was offended that I could no longer make posts like this because there was a group of people looking to be offended if they were made the slightest bit uncomfortable or not acknowledged on Mother's Day.

And all the while, I realized I was looking to be offended too. When I hopped on Facebook on Mother's Day, I was on the hunt to be offended, just knowing what *could* come. And I managed to see every post about a Mother's Day caveat as a personal attack. I was doing the very thing I had identified as way too sensitive in other people.

Being offendable is insanely easy. It stems from pride and from being unwilling to separate ourselves from what someone else is saying. We insert ourselves into every comment from a friend, every blog post, every grievance aired. We ask our-selves, *What does this mean to me? What does this say about me? How does this affect me?* We place ourselves at the center of something that likely has nothing to do with us. We assume the worst about others and struggle to find the grace to let go of our grudges, all while assuming the best about ourselves and somehow rationalizing each of our offenses.

I'm not here to justify the harsh things people have done or the way their comments have made you feel. I can't—there's a lot of evil and a lot of unfairness in the world. But I can encourage us to respond in a way that promotes grace and unity instead of dissension. If we choose not to be offended, even the greatest attempts by the devil to stir us toward anger and grumpiness will fail.

THE UPTIGHT REPUTATION

A few years ago, my sister, who was single at the time, was going to visit her friend who had just had a baby. She'd seen articles that said it's rude to visit the hospital, it's rude to visit at home, it's rude to not bring food, and it's rude to bring the wrong food. She was nervous that she would end up breaking the protocol. You have to bring food, you can't be late, and you shouldn't call or text too much. But what if you *are* running late? (Side note: According to the articles, you aren't allowed to run late because you aren't busy like a new mom is.) Do you text and try again another day? Did you miss the window? What do you do with all the food?

This pressure wasn't put on her by her friend but by a blur of the world's declarations. Each murmur. Each post. Each offense we feel we have to confront. These all add unnecessary noise and tension to the world of motherhood. So how do we let go? How do we live out a more heavenward approach in our everyday existence? The Bible offers this instruction: "Whoever covers an offense seeks love, but he who repeats a matter separates close friends" (Proverbs 17:9, ESV). I love how *The Message* puts this passage too: "Overlook an offense and bond a friendship; fasten on to a slight and—good-bye, friend!"

I am a justice girl. Strap a cape on me, and I will search the world over for anyone doing anything wrong and attempt to fix it. I want things to be right and accurate. I want to fix things that are broken. Okay, mostly *people* who are broken. Overlooking an offense seems pretty careless to me.

I might be able to convince myself on some days that this desire springs from a heart of justice, but in reality, it looks more like judging. It looks more like finding one more reason to decide someone isn't good enough to earn my precious time. So instead of holding fast to people, I hold tight to a slight.

I constantly need to be reminded of what God's Word says because it's easy to be disillusioned by the world's take on this. Scripture makes it clear that our readiness to be offended stops us from experiencing deep bonds in friendship. We let every little offense get under our skin, and it ends up separating us.

So let me grab my bullhorn (the kind conveniently shaped to curve right back to my own ears) and remind us all: WE'RE HUMAN. WE SAY DUMB THINGS. (I've probably said eleven thousand dumb things in this book alone . . . with hopefully one really wise thing? No? Okay. Let's move on.) There are just too many possible ways to be offended to start cutting people out of my life every time they offend me. This might make sense if there were perfect people running around, but there aren't (and I'm not perfect either). If we keep making cuts, we will be left as lonely, bitter mommas, surrounded by our slights.

Colossians 3:13 says, "Make allowance for each other's faults, and forgive anyone who offends you. Remember, the Lord forgave you, so you must forgive others." Basically, this means we need to plan ahead to forgive because we have all been royally forgiven for way bigger offenses than a short comment about the way we parent. We've been forgiven of every sin we ever have committed—and ever will commit. Jesus forgave the very people who nailed him to the cross, and I know full well that if I had been there, that would have included me, too.

God's forgiveness is the greatest gift we could ever receive.

Not only because it allows us to spend eternity with him but because it frees us from the prison of our own hurts. The fact that we are forgiven compels us to extend that same forgiveness to others. I can't help but feel refreshed in my mommy bones when I let go of that defensive comment and instead live out Colossians 3:13.

DO NOT QUARREL ON THE WAY

Thanks to six short words, I saw the story of Joseph and his brothers in a whole new light. You know the Joseph I'm talking about—the spoiled younger brother who didn't mind bragging about it and who eventually got sold into slavery by his brood of jealous brothers. Years passed, and he went from slave to the second most powerful guy in Egypt (God was totally involved, obviously). When he saw his brothers again and forgave them, Joseph sent them to get his father so he could see him after all that time.

Here were his parting words to them in Genesis 45:24: "Do not quarrel on the way" (ESV).

This line was referring to how they would tell this news to their father. They had just experienced huge forgiveness from this brother they had betrayed. He didn't want them to walk away cloaked in the sin he had just forgiven and then shift the blame. He was basically telling them, "This could tear you apart, but don't let it."

I think part of our tendency to take offense is a defense mechanism. If we decide to be offended first, we can't be blamed for offending anyone. We've painted ourselves as the victim, and anything we do to hurt someone else is justified because we were hurt first. It's kind of like if you want to punch someone—just get them to punch you first, and you can go out swinging in a blaze of glory instead of looking like an angry beast.

The problem is that living ready for a fight desensitizes us. We can't always be looking for a battle without becoming jaded in the way we see other people. We can't love well and forgive an offense if we train our eyes to find every little thing someone else does wrong.

So, mommas, I'm saying this to all of us: the offenses we take, the blame we want to put on others, the label of victim we want to put on ourselves, the chips we insist on carrying on our shoulders, the comments we want to read into too deeply, the judgment we want to pass on other parenting approaches—it will tear us apart, if we let it. So let's stop the habit of offense now. As believers, we are sisters in Christ, and we are all covered by the same grace. Not only our past failings but our future failings are nailed to the cross. We have to stop trying to pull other people's failures down from the cross just so we can find something to be offended by.

A BETTER REPUTATION

There is a better way: "Sensible people control their temper; they earn respect by overlooking wrongs" (Proverbs 19:11). As we exercise patience and control our tempers, God gets the glory and we point other people to him. When we could take offense but don't, that speaks volumes about where our value and confidence come from.

It's possible to tip the scales: we can give little weight to an offense from people while giving tremendous weight to the words of God. God gets the glory in those moments when we overlook an offense, which I'd say is way better than feeling temporarily vindicated here on earth.

One of the keys to being able to let go of an offense is to have a teachable spirit. To be teachable, we have to be open to the idea that we aren't perfect and we don't know it all. In contrast, if our immediate response is offense, we forfeit the chance to change and grow.

Let me share a small example. I spent a stubborn year or so being miserable every time someone said my new baby girl looked exactly like my husband and nothing like me. If I had to hear one more time that this little baby I'd spent *ten months* uncomfortably carrying around and then had cut out of my belly didn't look a thing like me, I was going to cry. The more the comments kept coming, the more frustrated I became. I was convinced that everyone else was the problem, and I refused to entertain the idea that I should just change my attitude about it. I was too focused on the offense and waiting for everyone else to change.

Eventually I did change my attitude. It took a long time—maybe two years. By that point, I had forgotten about the morning sickness, the constant discomfort of pregnancy, and the breastfeeding—oh, the breastfeeding. As I gained some distance from that season, I started to realize how ridiculous it is to be offended when other people think your child looks like the man you love. When I was open to being teachable instead of focusing on my sacrifices, I was able to remind myself that people weren't implying that I wasn't Vivi's mom or that I hadn't devoted most of the last ten months to her needs. They were simply saying she had Tyler's features. Exercising those thoughts helped me to be more rational and look at people's intentions instead of reacting out of a victim mentality.

On the other end of the spectrum, maybe it's not that we need to be offended less but that we simply need to say less. Y'all, this is me. I want to take care of everyone, especially my sister and my husband. I'm afraid that if I don't say everything, God won't be able to get his message to them. It's rather conceited of me, no? But when I am forced to embrace reality (read, when my mentor asks me the tough questions), this is what shakes out.

In *Ordering Your Private World*, Gordon MacDonald says, "One does wonder if we have simply talked too much in our books and magazine articles—told each other too much when we should have reserved the conversation for God alone."[2] This quote is certainly convicting to share *in a book I'm writing*, but believe me, what I'm sharing is only about a tenth of what I think I should share.

Lately God has been showing me that not everything I learn needs to be shared. As someone whose job it is to create content to inspire others, I have been a little slow in learning this. But I'm starting to realize that sometimes thoughts pass through me before they really take root. I'm so bent on producing content for others that I don't let it do its full work in me first.

Sharing information isn't a bad thing. We just need to return to the starting point. Where are our hearts? What are our motives? And to go even deeper, have we really processed this ourselves, or are we spitting out half-chewed thoughts?

In a world of open letters and quick reflexes, how precious to have some things that we sift through slowly and keep just between us and God.

ACTION STEPS

1. **Imagine yourself saying the same thing that offended you.** When someone says something that offends you, try to picture the same words coming out of your own mouth. Could you justify it if you had to defend yourself? If someone is driving too fast, they're reckless, but if we're

driving too fast, we call the other person a moron for not knowing how to drive. We can make a case for anything for ourselves—can we have the same kind of grace for others?

2. **Remember your reputation.** I don't mean this in a superficial way but as a reminder that we are ambassadors of Christ and we want to represent him well. This might sound trite, but the application still holds value: What would Jesus do?

3. **If the offense is small, let it go. If it's big, acknowledge it and deal with it, and then let it go.** Trying to push down a major offense can make it worse. We don't have to pretend it never happened. But once we've worked through it, we can choose to forgive, knowing that God has forgiven us way more.

KEY VERSE

Whoever covers an offense seeks love, but he who repeats a matter separates close friends.

PROVERBS 17:9, ESV

PRAYER

Father, give me the gift of being able to let go of things and not take them so personally. I don't want to waste my energy being offended. I don't want to be bitter and on guard. Help me to see the selfishness in demanding that everyone behave the way I think they should. Give me a heart that longs to understand before being understood. And please give me the wisdom to know when to speak and when to stay quiet. In Jesus' name, amen.

Chapter 17

OTHER MOMMIES
MADE ME DO IT

Say Hello to Breathing Room

I THINK ANY MOM WITH A BOX of Legos in the house has longed for minimalism at some point. It's not just me, right? I quickly feel outnumbered by the army of little blocks and threaten to take them all to the garbage if they don't get in line or back in the box. They seem to clutter my mind as well as my floor, and before long the idea of minimalism sounds as therapeutic as a scalp massage.

The idea of margin—the white space in our schedules, homes, and mind—sounds like an oxymoron when you combine it with motherhood. I remember when I first learned about this idea. Ironically, it was when my first daughter was four months old. Fresh on the heels of a whole new world of responsibilities, I found the idea of margin irresistible. I made a few pivotal changes and was amazed that with an infant I was experiencing more peace and space in my life than I'd had before kids.

But practicing margin is like using a muscle. If we neglect it for too long, it loses strength. And in spite of our best intentions, the presence of other mommas can distract us and convince us that we need *extra* extracurricular activities, all the educational toys, and Instagram-worthy moments. Because of that, I want to share some practical advice to help us change our thought patterns so we can go from desperately striving for more to embracing the incredible blessing of margin and limits.

Let's start with minimalism. It's not just a buzzword that makes me feel euphoric when I think of it. It's an action word. Joshua Becker calls minimalism "the intentional promotion of the things we most value and removing anything that distracts us from it."[1] The abundance of extra doesn't just take up space. It keeps us from the things we want to be a part of our lives.

In 2 Timothy, Paul tells Timothy that Demas has left him because he was "in love with this present world" (4:10, ESV). His love for the present world distracted him from his true purpose. This is like jumping back into prison after we've been told we're free to go. Our love for the world keeps us stuck in overspending, overeating, overindulging in Netflix and screen time, overanalyzing and filling our minds with worry and fear, and obsessing over good things. We've been set free from all this, yet we put on our handcuffs again on a daily basis. We may think loving the present world is harmless, but it's not. It pulls us away from the Lord and the plans he has for us.

Matthew 6:33 gives us clear direction on how to handle the here and now: "Seek the Kingdom of God above all else, and live righteously, and he will give you everything you need."

Even the seemingly big, legitimate concerns shouldn't occupy our hearts and minds more than pursuing God's Kingdom. Not because they don't matter, but because God will take care of them. He doesn't need us to micromanage him.

This quote by Hannah Anderson stopped me in my tracks: "When we disregard our natural human limitations, we set ourselves in God's place."[2] I know I'm not God. Not by a long shot. But if you're asking if I try to push for more and more and if I expect to do superhuman things sometimes, if you're asking if I heap extra onto an already-packed space on the calendar and just expect to make it work, if you're asking if I eat too much junk "because I deserve it" and then by some random coincidence don't feel my best, if you're asking if I feel guilty for failing at things God never expected me to do, well then . . .

Guilty. As. Charged.

It's time to stop daydreaming about getting a few extra hours in our day. When I remember that I have limited resources and time, I'm able to take some of the pressure off myself. I can accept the fact that I'm not Superwoman. Which apparently is news only to me.

UNFINISHED DREA . . .

One day when I was driving and mentally planning my to-do list for the day, I became overwhelmed by feelings of anxiety, hurry, and frustration. I asked myself, *What am I even trying to accomplish?* As I was pondering this, the thought that we dare not admit crossed my mind: *If I didn't have kids, I could get so much more done!*

As soon as the thought formed in my mind, I felt ridiculous. Why was I striving to accomplish all these dreams at the expense of my kids? Raising my girls is far more worthy of my time than completing my projects, organizing my house to a T, and reading a million books. Don't get me wrong—I want to use my gifts for God. But am I trying to accomplish too much? Am I trying to complete more than he intended for me? Am I trying to do things that don't even matter by his standards?

Peter Scazzero says, "We will finish our lives with unfinished goals and dreams."[3] In other words, we aren't bound to some predetermined list of things we have to finish before we die. Most of us don't go through life striving for an end-all-be-all finish line—this is all happening in our subconscious. Under the surface, we feel like we're going to arrive at some ending point, even though that's not possible this side of heaven. So let's take the pressure off. No matter how old we are when we die, there will be things we'll leave undone. We'll never reach "done," so we can stop striving so hard for something we'll never actually attain. This should liberate us, not discourage us.

Life is a marathon, not a sprint. I wonder if this is a big reason we're all so worn out. I know next to nothing about running, but I do know this: marathon runners and sprinters run differently. They also go into the race with a different mindset. If a marathoner sets their pace the way a sprinter does, they will burn out and lose the race.

Mommas, we face a lot of obstacles in this marathon called life. Let's address four specific areas that challenge our margin and figure out how to combat them.

UNENDING COMPARISON

One of the greatest roadblocks to finding margin is clumping together what every other mom is doing and then using that information as our personal to-do list. If you follow one hundred moms on Instagram, talk to five neighbors with kids, get to know four parents at school, and do life with three of your siblings, that can make for a pretty overwhelming master plan. We simply weren't created to do it all.

Case in point: on the second picture day of the school year, I decided, *No $65 school pictures today.* Once a year was enough. But when the car attendant came to get Vivi from the carpool line and asked if she'd be getting her picture taken, I felt big-time momma guilt. To make matters worse, Vivi was wearing a shirt she'd worn a million times, and she didn't have all the picture-day accessories. I'm betting her unbrushed hair was what prompted the car attendant's question in the first place. I worried about how Vivi might stand out and, maybe even more so, what others would think of me as a mom.

We long for margin, but those invisible pressures keep piling on us. Thank you, Jesus, that there wasn't a Gap next door to her school so I couldn't suddenly decide, "Yeaaaaah. She's getting her picture taken. I forgot her outfit—let me go grab it." Nope, there was no turning back. I was alone with my thoughts, feeling like the worst mom ever. It didn't help when I remembered that the shorts she was wearing were covered in either preexisting stains or food from breakfast—I couldn't tell which.

Comparison isn't harmful just because it makes us feel like garbage. It's also damaging because of the way it influences our actions. Comparison can sideline us from our own mission when we start feeling responsible to do things God has called other people to do. And the thing is, God doesn't give out extra credit if we finish our mission and start working on someone else's. We please God and glorify him most when we listen intently for his leading and obey him. Isn't that refreshing?

God doesn't cram things in, so I know his mission for us, if we choose to accept it, will be a breath of fresh air compared to what we might attempt on our own.

Proverbs 4:25-26 says, "Look straight ahead, and fix your eyes on what lies before you. Mark out a straight path for your feet; stay on the safe path." When we run our own races, the competition and comparison melt away. What's left is a simple, straight vision ahead of us.

UNLIMITED OPTIONS

I've spent many an hour searching for products online. Whether it is a dress for a particular occasion, a piece of furniture for a specific spot in our home, or the perfect photo to accompany a blog post, the World Wide Web makes it possible to spend six hours searching for something and still not find what you want. The reason? There's always something more out there. Sometimes the unknown stirs up discontentment in us and keeps us endlessly searching. We're convinced that the best option is right around the corner, and we're terrified that if we give up the search too early, we'll pick the wrong thing.

The fear and weariness that come from having too many choices is known as decision fatigue. According to Wikipedia (yes, I'm about to quote Wikipedia), this is defined as "the deteriorating quality of decisions made by an individual after a long session of decision making. It is now understood as one of the causes of irrational trade-offs in decision making."[4]

It may seem counterintuitive, but when we eliminate some options, we make better decisions. Each new option costs us something. In other words, limits are good. When we can turn certain decisions into habits, this autopilot approach frees up our energy so we can make the really important decisions. You've likely heard that Steve Jobs wore the same outfit (a black turtleneck) every day to work. I don't think he did this because he was a boring guy; I think he did it to save his creative genius for bigger decisions.

Imagine what our lives would look like if we created self-imposed limits when it comes to certain decisions. What if we said something like this: *I shop at the little boutique on Main Street, Gap, and Target for my clothes. If I don't find stuff there, I do without it.* That might sound a bit restricting. But deep down, I feel a sense of relief when my search has boundary lines. It has a definitive end. Now, that's not to say that if I randomly see the perfect dress in a store window, I'm not allowed to get it. It just means I'm free from the unlimited search that can wear me thin.

I recently did an experiment to limit the decisions in my morning routine. Sometimes I get overwhelmed with figuring out what to read next in my Bible and which book to read (since I'm normally reading several books at a time). The night before, I wrote down what I was going to read in my Bible and what book I was going to read in the morning. Y'all. This was such a small thing, but it saved me brain space that I usually spend procrastinating. I was able to use that time to go deep and read more than usual.

UNMANAGEABLE STUFF

Life is not derived from stuff. Luke 12:15 captures these words of Jesus: "Watch out and guard yourselves against every form of greed; for not even when one has an overflowing abundance does his life consist of nor is it derived from his possessions" (AMP). We know that life is more than stuff, but we still find ourselves on an endless search to fill our lives with more of it. Have you ever strolled through the dollar section of Target thinking, *Do I "need" anything?* You can't think of anything you need, but you look anyway, wondering if there's something you forgot you needed. Is this irony, or what? If we can forget we need something, maybe it's not an actual need.

Stuff can have an odd control over our lives. I feel it when I get stuff I've ordered online. Suddenly I'm spending what could be playtime with the girls opening packages, breaking down boxes for recycling, putting new things where they need to go, trying on clothes, repacking things that need to be returned, and trying to figure out when I can return said items. I think I own this stuff, but before long, this stuff is controlling me.

Joshua Becker opened my eyes to the real issue of the rich young ruler in Matthew 19.[5] The man goes to Jesus and asks what he can do to be saved. Jesus tells him to sell his possessions and follow him. The rich young ruler goes away grieving because he doesn't want to give up his things. The man says no because he sees this act as a sacrifice. He doesn't see the worth of eternal life compared to his possessions. I am tempted to call him a moron for not grasping what really matters, but I do the same thing. What we sacrifice in an effort to not sacrifice our things is memories with our kids or meaningful conversations with our husband. We may even sacrifice a calling that doesn't pay much for a job that makes us more money so we can buy more stuff. I shudder to think how our hunger for more forces us to work longer hours on things that God never asked us to do.

I desperately want to see letting go of my things as an invitation instead of a sacrifice.

UNRELENTING GRIND

In an overwhelmingly busy season, when I was just starting to grow my first business, I wanted to figure out what I could delegate or get rid of. On a sheet of paper, I made two lists: "Things I Love to Do" and "Things That Stress Me Out." As I started writing, I realized something odd. I had almost the same list on both sides. How was that possible? As I pondered my lists, the determining factor became clear: how full my life was at the time. The things we love can become the things that stress us out when we have too much.

I'm constantly trying to add good things to my life. That's a fine inclination, as long as I remember to imagine the full picture and not isolate each aspect of my life. For example, writing a book is a really good thing. Writing a book while in my first trimester of pregnancy is not a good thing (for me, at least). Leading a small group is a really good thing. Leading a small group that keeps me from investing in my neighbors who always hang out during that time may not be the best thing.

When we make decisions, we need to recognize that each one requires some sort of trade-off. That's why it helps to think through this a bit before we commit to something. What are we okay missing out on? I've wrestled with this a lot, because there are so many things I want to do. If I say yes to too many commitments, the trade-off will be an impatient mom. And with a toddler, let's be honest—I need all the patience I can muster right now.

OVERWHELMING LOOPS

That feeling of being overwhelmed can be paralyzing. Here's a recent example from my own life. I was aimlessly scrolling through the Bermuda Triangle of my phone: (1) Instagram, (2) e-mails, (3) Facebook. Repeat. I knew that work and chores were piling up around me and that I should get up, but instead I'd loop back through again and again. Thirty minutes later,

I was so frustrated for giving in to the overwhelmed feeling. And guess what? That left me even more overwhelmed.

The natural tendency is for overwhelmed feelings to breed more overwhelmed feelings. As the stuff piles high, we feel like we can't start decluttering because there's too much. We can't clear off our calendars because it will require us to e-mail five people to tell them no, and that feels like a lot of work. The only way out is to take that first hard step and break the pattern. Elisabeth Elliot says, "When in the face of powerful temptation to do wrong, there is the swift, hard renunciation—*I will not*—it will be followed by the sudden loosing of the bonds of self, the yes to God that lets in sunlight, sets us singing and all freedom's bells clanging for joy."[6]

There is such hope and power in knowing that the bondage we feel can be loosened as we make one simple choice to break the cycle. What is one small decision you can make today to loosen the bonds of a stuffed-to-the-gills life?

————————

ACTION STEPS

1. **Create a "Things I Don't Do" list.** There is something really liberating about knowing what we aren't going to worry about doing. It takes practice to say no, but the more we do it, the more our "no muscle" will grow and the more we'll be okay not doing it all. What you don't do is as important as what you do. Celebrate this! Here are some items on my list: we don't go to many birthday parties and showers, I don't dress my kids to a T, I don't dye my hair (that may change soon), I don't DIY or do crafts. (Note that we are all different, so our lists will be

different too. Some of the things on my "don't do" list may be things that are life giving to you.)

2. **Recognize the things that cause you to feel over-whelmed.** If you are left feeling like you have tons to do every time you're on Pinterest, stop pinning. It sounds so simple, but we forget that we can choose not to do certain things. As you find yourself overwhelmed, stop and really think about the source, and then have the confidence to set limitations that make sense for you and your family.

3. **Redefine "need."** This word has basically lost its meaning. When we're going through Target and my daughter says she "needs" princess Band-Aids, I think she sounds ridiculous. She has some at home, and even if she didn't, she'd survive just fine without Belle wrapped around her ant bite for all of five minutes that she keeps it on. I recognize how silly this sounds when it comes to Vivi's whims, but I rarely recognize how ridiculous I sound when I tell my husband or even God what I "need." If you find yourself in a spot where you feel like you need something to be content, I encourage you to ask yourself bluntly, *Do I really require this for my existence?* If the answer is no, add it to the "nice to have" column and then weigh those items as well. How much life would this bring to you? For example, patio furniture is not something we need, but it has sure added lots of joy to our lives as we get to enjoy our porch daily. However, if I'm being honest with myself, I have a bit more trouble convincing myself that a random new shirt will add joy to my life.

4. **Make a habit of pruning.** Pruning is simply reevaluating different areas of life and deciding what to get rid of. This might mean looking at all your family's commitments

and seeing if they still serve you. Or it might be as practical as removing clothes that no longer fit from your kids' closets. I'm a ruthless pruner, but I still find myself in crazy seasons when I look around and think, *How did this happen?* The natural tendency is to accumulate more and more, not less and less, so we have to be intentional about coming back to this habit regularly.

KEY VERSE

Look straight ahead, and fix your eyes on what lies before you. Mark out a straight path for your feet; stay on the safe path.

PROVERBS 4:25-26

PRAYER

Father, help me to dig into my own life and forget about what every other mom is doing or not doing. Forgive me for placing expectations on myself that you never intended. Instead, help me to embrace the limits you set on me. Show me how to add white space to my life instead of cramming in so much that the good stuff spills out. Prompt me when it's time to prune, and give me peace to do so without mommy guilt. In Jesus' name, amen.

Chapter 18

PUT YOUR SHOES ON!

Say Hello to Slowing Down

IT'S ALL TOO COMMON for one of these phrases to be heard at any given moment in my house:

· "Hurry up and put on your shoes!"
· "Hurry up and finish dinner!"
· "Hurry up and get in the car!"
· "Hurry, hurry, hurry!"

I don't have any research to back this up, but I think words like these are likely heard in your home too. *Busy* is more than a buzzword. It's the war of our generation. And the battle cry is "Hurry up!" How else could we possibly get our little troop moving without that phrase, which we draw like a sword at a moment's notice?

I try to fight the hurry, because I'm a rebel like that, but many days I succumb to it. My soul longs for a slower pace. If you've ever felt like *busy* is a four-letter word, you're not alone. I've been there too. And I'm pretty sure I've avoided the word more than I avoid some real four-letter words.

But did you know there's a difference between *busyness* and *hurry*? Our culture would have us believe we can't feel anything but hurried because life is so busy. But this is a lie we have to reject. It turns out that our souls can be at peace regardless of the pace around us. From the last chapter, you know that even when we try to carve out margin in our lives, we can't control our schedules totally. And really, there's something much more dangerous than a busy life.

In *Soul Keeping*, John Ortberg draws a rather freeing contrast between *busy* and *hurried*. Busy has to do with what's happening on the outside, while hurry has to do with what's happening on the inside. The biggest hindrance to peace is not a full calendar or physically demanding tasks but a spirit that is distracted and disconnected from the Lord.

I'll gladly take some "busy" if it doesn't automatically exile me to hurry. Our challenge is to stop trying *just* to solve the problem of busyness and identify where we are hurried instead. If we can solve this riddle, we will have peace even in the midst of busy seasons. On the flip side, we can live an unbusy life that still has a pace of hurry in the soul.

When we recognize that time is something to be enjoyed rather than something to be rationed, it will change the way we see the world. How much more would I enjoy the moment if I weren't trying to pass it off to the highest bidder? How much more would I enjoy the moment if I saw it as a gift? That might sound cliché. *Every moment we have is a gift.* Barf. I get it. I might as well tell you to see the glass as half full. But as I frantically attempt to finish writing a certain number of words before my unpredictable napper wakes up,

I'm realizing that I miss out when I have a death grip on fitting every single thing in.

So instead of starting with a full calendar that overwhelms my soul, I want to be intentional about adding each item on my to-do list with joy. Even the laundry. Lord help me on that one, but even the laundry is a gift. When I can see each moment as a gift instead of a rationed resource I must squeeze every drop from, Grumpy Mom can take a much-needed holiday. She's been busy lately.

THE MAIL NEVER STOPS

The cost of not slowing down and becoming still is steep. In fact, God talked about the importance of rest in his top-ten list (see Exodus 20). That's the biblical side of things, but you may have heard it in another form on *Seinfeld*.

Newman: I'm a United States postal worker.

George: Aren't those the guys that always go crazy? . . .

Newman: Sometimes . . .

Seinfeld: Why is that?

Newman: Because the mail never stops. It just keeps coming and coming and coming; there's never a letup. It's relentless. Every day it piles up more and more and more! And you gotta get it out, but the more you get it out, the more it keeps coming in. And then the bar code reader breaks and it's Publisher's Clearing House day!

This example is hilarious and painful at the same time—partly because this isn't true just for those who hustle packages by trade. I could say the same thing about laundry. It just keeps coming and coming and coming—there's never a letup. Every day it piles up more and more! And you have to get it out, but the more you get it out, the more it keeps coming in. Then lice hits! And then the stomach bug, and then it's picture day!

It's enough to make any mom feel a little cuckoo. Why? Because we simply were not designed to live in overdrive.

When I was growing up, my mom was a fast driver. It came from years of running late. She will tell you that the hurry affected not only her driving; it affected the pace of her heart as well. The emergency mode stopped being temporary. It became the new normal even when she got off the road. After years of this mentality, she could no longer take the stress and she finally decided it was time for a change. It took years for her to realize it, but once she did, she was able to break the cycle and be set free from hurry.

If we don't make the choice to slow down, there are bound to be consequences at some point. Do you feel slightly off kilter? Like you can't think straight? Is your health taking a nosedive? Have you accepted these things as a normal part of being a mom?

I once read that the Chinese character for busyness is made by joining two characters into a single pictograph: heart and killing.[1] This makes me wince. There's no beating around the bush, no excuses about how there are some exceptions and I probably fall perfectly into them. Busyness, which in this sense seems to refer to the hurry in our souls, is "heart killing."

STOP PUTTING UP CHAIRS

In her book *Present Over Perfect*, Shauna Niequist tells the story of two pastors. The younger one tells the older one that his church just kept growing, even beyond what he wanted and beyond what he felt he could handle. The older pastor matter-of-factly says that he must have wanted it to keep growing. The young pastor disagrees and emphasizes that he had nothing to do with it. The older one says, "You kept putting up more chairs."[2]

In my mind-set that always seeks something bigger, better, and faster, I am left thinking, *What should the pastor have done? Turned people away? Let people be uncomfortable?* He had no alternative but to put up more chairs. Right?

This perspective may be precisely why our lives are over-run by commitments that shouldn't be priorities. We won't do the uncomfortable business of making tough decisions. In the moment, it feels easier to say yes than to entertain a tough question and address it. I'm not talking about having a good, full calendar that is life giving. I'm talking about being over-committed with soul-sucking activities.

I recently went through a really dry season, when I felt like I was just reacting to everything instead of living on purpose. I was beyond weary. Even bone weary didn't speak to the depth of how I felt. The word that kept coming to mind was *brittle*— I was sure I would crack with the slightest pressure. And let's be honest—I was also way past grumpy.

Let's go back to the story of those two pastors. As I play this scenario out further and try to figure out a solution, here's what I see happening. The people who aren't willing to stand go home or find another church. The people who are willing to stand—the ones who stick around—are incredibly devoted. The church is stronger because the people who stay are the ones who desperately want to be there, even if the environment isn't perfect. The ones who stick it out are the ones who are willing to volunteer and invest in the future of the church. The ones who prioritize their own comfort, the ones who are looking for an easy church to go to, the ones looking for a church that will serve them left a long time ago. In the end, the church is stronger because the pastor didn't put up more chairs.

The process can be messy and even a little ugly for a while. This is a lesson I learned from crepe myrtle trees.

I know next to nothing about gardening, but what I do know is that crepe myrtles, a South Louisiana staple, should get cut back to ugly stumps every year. If you saw all the limbs hacked away in early spring, you might assume the tree was dead and be tempted to uproot it. But according to my mom, this is done *on purpose*. This sounds very much like a setback to me. And yes, it may look ridiculous for a little while, but it's the very thing that keeps the tree blooming year after year.

What keeps us in a constant flurry of hurry instead of enjoying slow, steady growth? What looks good now but will likely kill some aspect of our lives before the next season rolls around? These are the things we need to prune from our lives.

THE TIME I GOT WHAT I WANTED

I was on hold with the IRS (always a delight), catching up on the latest political gossip online, checking in on a Facebook group, and feeding my youngest her pureed zucchini, cauliflower, and mango. I was also writing this chapter of the book. All at once I felt convicted about doing more than an octopus would feel comfortable with. So I said goodbye to Facebook and politics for the moment. My pace slowed down instantly—this was what I wanted, right? But I kept twitching, reaching for my computer to occupy the space I'd just made so I could slow down.

Here are some uncomfortable realities about our lives of hurry:

1. **If we keep a hurried pace for long enough, the slow pace of life seems boring.** There, I said it. Sometimes I need a little more action in my life. I don't actually like slowness. As much as I talk about wanting to get rid of hurry, when I manage to do that, I find out that I kind of prefer hurry. When I get a taste of slowing down, it feels uncomfortable and makes me reach for anything that will stimulate all my senses at once. But this is not a signal that we should keep hurrying; this is a reminder that slowing down requires a complete shift. Just because hurry feels okay in the moment doesn't mean slowing down isn't worth pursuing. The process of deconditioning ourselves from hurry will likely be uncomfortable, so we're going to need to get comfy with some discomfort. But the result will be worth it. My family recently spent some time away with the express purpose of resting after a really busy season. The first few days were pure torture because we had grown so accustomed to a fast pace. But by the last day, the slowness had refreshed me more than anything I'd ever experienced.

2. **Sometimes we multitask not because we have to but because we want to.** We think that if we hurry enough now, even when it isn't required, we'll make up time on the back end, when it counts. Sister, it counts now. I'm the chief offender on this one. Efficiency is my love language. No, really. If you want to show me love,

do so with the least amount of time and the biggest return on investment. I don't see slow moments as beautiful moments; I see them as inefficient. I'm trying to retrain my brain to stop seeing slow moments as liabilities and instead see them as moments of peaceful concentration that will save my sanity. Not only that, but living this way looks a little more like Jesus, who was never in a hurry.

3. **Sometimes we're looking for quantity over quality.** Of course I want quality, but can you make it double? As in, quality in large quantities? I am looking for too much quality, and it turns out that I get drowned by the water hose I've strapped to my mouth. And as silly as it is, I'm so used to the water hose that it sounds downright exhausting to sip out of a straw. As you can see, I still have a lot of deconditioning to do.

TAKE "TAKING THINGS SLOW" SLOW

How do we slow down when we don't really want to? The answer: we have to take "taking things slow" slow. Makes perfect sense, right?

I don't have this all figured out yet, but I'm trying to battle the hurry by making small adjustments. I've started reflecting more on my days. When I journal in the evenings, it forces me to stop and look back—something that will give you whiplash when you're running full-steam ahead. This is not a new idea; there's an ancient prayerful approach of reflecting on our days. It's called the Examen Prayer.

In a nutshell (because I *give* efficiency as a love language too!), this prayer method, inspired by Saint Ignatius, includes God in our review of the day. We play back our day like a movie, but with special attention to God being next to us. There are five basic parts to this prayer.

1. Walk through the day and express gratitude for all God has done.
2. Take a moment to ask the Lord to fill you with his Spirit so you can hear what he wants you to hear.
3. Imagine watching a screen of your day, with the Lord watching beside you.
4. Recognize the areas where you messed up, but don't dwell on them too much. Release them to God.
5. Look at what you learned and picture the next day and how you can do things differently.[3]

As I have tried to slow down my days, this reflective practice has helped me to slow down my hands and my heart as well. When we spend so much energy trying to survive the day or we spin our wheels trying to make things happen for ourselves, our lives pass us by. We go to bed Sunday night with the highest hopes of starting that new fitness regimen or healthy habit. Then we blink and it's Thursday, and we've completely forgotten our intention. This leaves us feeling even more rushed. We are officially behind and playing catch-up before we even get started. This becomes a chronic feeling— a constant nagging that what we've done is never enough.

I think that's why I've found such freedom in my nightly review of the day with God. This simple five to ten minutes reminds me that I'm human and a work in progress. My daily check-in sets a new, steady pace that isn't as volatile as my usual revved-up Sunday nights and whiplash-inducing days. I don't expect so much out of each day, but at the same time, I'm appreciating the one-degree shifts my heart makes each day. And with a year of this incremental change, 365 degrees later, I could be a transformed person.

It turns out that life doesn't pass us by as much when we take the time to actually look at it.

LIFE IS IN THE JOURNEY

We can live with a journey mentality or a destination mentality. If we believe that life is about the journey, we can find contentment and enjoy the process. If we believe that life is about the destination, we'll never be satisfied and we'll be filled with regret. We can't be rushing toward something in the future *and* be content with the present at the same time.

Here are some questions to ask yourself to gauge whether you're living in the present:

- Am I working for the weekend, or am I able to enjoy the work I'm doing on a regular old Tuesday?
- Am I clamoring for the day when nursing won't hurt and my stitches are healed, or am I able to enjoy the first weeks with a newborn?
- Am I longing for the school year to start so I can get some free time, or am I enjoying the laid-back pace of summer with my kids?
- Am I waiting to swim in the pool with my kids until I'm in better shape, or am I embracing the body I have in this moment?

If we are constantly waiting for the destination, we won't be able to relax. We won't be comfortable until we arrive. And the crazy part is, we'll never arrive, because the finish line keeps moving. This realization should freak me out, but it's rather freeing. If the destination I'm trying to reach is unattainable anyway, then why not just slow down?

Jeremiah 2:25 says, "Slow down. Take a deep breath. What's the hurry? Why wear yourself out? Just what are you after anyway?" (MSG). It's time to stop striving and start embracing what's right in front of us. The spot we're in right now may have been a destination we dreamed of years ago.

Grumpy Mom thrives on hurry, so she'll be rendered helpless as we slow down and relish the good right in front of us.

ACTION STEPS

1. **Cut back on "hurries."** Once I started paying attention, I realized how often I said *hurry*. There are definitely moments that require us to move quickly, but I've tried to cut back on saying "Hurry!" to my girls whenever possible. This has helped slow me down, and it's helping me learn patience, too, which I can always use an extra helping of.

2. **Reflect on the day with the Lord.** Save the last ten minutes of the evening to review your day in prayer. Can't give ten minutes? Just ask yourself, *How's my soul today? What am I after, anyway?*

3. **Move to-do items off your list once work/nap time is over.** In the past, if I had to-do items left over, I used to try to cram them in after the girls woke up from their nap. I was in a constant state of frustration as I tried to squeeze in one last e-mail or one more decluttering project. Now as soon as work time is over, I move the undone items to another day. It's been freeing to spend

the remainder of my day not feeling chronically behind and like I need to do more.

4. **Get moving.** Physically moving our bodies when our hearts are filled with hurry is an effective outlet for getting rid of restlessness. Sometimes we are most restless because we feel like we're standing still or being slowed down. Sometimes we truly need to slow down and rest. Other times we need to take a break from what we're doing and get some energy out, like a kindergarten class midway through a phonics lesson.

KEY VERSE

Slow down. Take a deep breath. What's the hurry? Why wear yourself out? Just what are you after anyway?

JEREMIAH 2:25, MSG

PRAYER

Lord, slow me down. Set my pace and my heartbeat to yours. So often I try to run ahead of you, and in the process, I make wrong turns that set me back. Shield me from the thinking that I need to be doing something productive at all times, and remind me that your love for me doesn't depend on what I accomplish. In Jesus' name, amen.

Chapter 19

GETTING MOMMA'S ATTENTION

Say Hello to Living in the Moment

I REMEMBER THE FIRST CONVERSATION I had with my mentor. I was so excited to share with her all the areas I wanted to work on. I was even excited to get her advice about how I could improve my life. As we sat on my porch on an unseasonably warm winter day, sipping tea, I had an unspoken plan about what needed my attention.

After I shared a bit about my life, she asked if I struggled with being too driven. I'm not sure if the waterworks started right then, but I felt exposed. I was aware of the issue, but having someone diagnose the problem so quickly made me feel vulnerable. We made lemonade, though. The conversation challenged me to address the issue out loud with a real human being instead of in my ongoing internal dialogue: *I should really slow down and be more present, but I'm too busy now.*

I bet you've had a similar inner dialogue. This seems to be

the heart's desire of our generation. We all long to be present in a world of distractions, but we struggle as we navigate how to do that. All around us, moms are on their phones staring at pictures of their babies while the very same faces are unfiltered and in full color right in front of them. Or they're checking e-mail, hoping for a big break so they can work less and enjoy those kids who are patiently waiting for their attention right now. I know about this firsthand because I do it too.

PEOPLE OVER PRODUCTIVITY

In my attempt to tame the beast of distracted motherhood, I wrote down this goal: "Today I'm going to prioritize people over productivity." Soon after writing these words, I found myself faced with a choice. I could visit my grandmother, or I could get ahead on that mound of laundry that was piling up. Normally I would choose the laundry. Without hesitation. I love my grandma, I really do, but I usually tell myself that doing the laundry will keep my life on track. It will make for less chaos in the evening and less hustle in the morning as we all try to find the right socks. Judging by my typical choices, I love productivity more than I love people.

On this day, though, I chose Grandma. And seeing her face light up with joy as she watched the girls, I knew I'd made the right choice. This should have been obvious to me already, but it became clear that day: people matter more than productivity!

If you aren't a type A, you may be wondering, *Why the exclamation point?* This is old news, right? But if you're like me, you probably need this reminder. When I have my own list of what's important, I tend to forget what's important to God. My list can include a lot of good things, like a clean house, folded laundry, completed scrapbooks, or a healthy diet. We can put a lot of emphasis on getting these things right for our kids, and they're great goals, but if they are replacing soul-deep moments with our kids, these items aren't worth it. Our kids need our presence more than they need a lot of the things we prioritize.

Maybe it's time to set our lists aside and start focusing on God's list.

When I attempt to accomplish my priorities along with God's, Grumpy Mom starts knocking on the door. When I take on more than God intended, I might as well set up the guest room for her, because she's going to be around for a while. My people will end up with the short end of the stick. And since it's easier to ask for grace from our families than from people we don't know as well, strangers and acquaintances can get our best time while our families get the leftovers.

Here's a challenging question to ask ourselves as our heads hit the pillow each night: "From the way I lived my life today, would my highest praise come from my husband and children?"[1] This question cuts deep. Many days my highest praise comes from Instagram comments and e-mails from customers. Thankfully, though, the nightly routine of asking this question of myself is taking root. I'm recognizing that the things I normally do so casually are in fact making impressions on my children. When Vivi insists on bringing my phone to me because it's a whole room's length away, I'm embarrassed. Even at the ripe old age of four, she perceives how much I need it.

I've noticed that during really full seasons, when I'm distracted physically or mentally, my kids tend to act out. It's like clockwork—as my time present with them goes down, the tantrums rise. When my mind is distracted by a thousand different things, my kids' demands seem to interrupt my inner dialogue. I want to reverse that. Instead, I want to recognize that my inner dialogue is interrupting my time with my kids. This releases them from the burden of trying to live silently until spoken to while momma has all these thoughts.

If there was ever someone who was fully present with people, it was Jesus. As we start to tally up all the legitimate reasons we're distracted, can we imagine the inner dialogue he must have had? The responsibilities that must have weighed on him? The pressure he must have felt? Peter Scazzero says, "Jesus was secure in his Father's love, in himself, and thus was able to withstand enormous pressure."[2]

We tend to think we aren't present because of external things, like the fact that our phones are packed with so many distractions. But I think the reality goes deeper than that. We are distracted by the lies we believe that draw us to our phones in the first place. Maybe it's the pressure to be in the know about current events or the belief that we need to see every post by our favorite ministry. It might be a sinking feeling that life isn't enough and that maybe our purpose can be found on the other side of a screen. If we are truly secure in God's love, we can resist the pull of whatever is sidetracking us. And just like Jesus, we can be okay with disappointing people sometimes, knowing our security is not in the opinions of the world but in God and his perfect plan for our lives.

THE GUILT CYCLE

Some days while I'm working, I have a nagging feeling that I should be with my kids. And when I'm with my kids, I feel like I should be working. My friend Michelle calls this the "guilt cycle." And it's a vicious one, because the guilt distracts us and makes us feel bad for not doing what we think we should be doing, so when we switch gears to the next thing, we're left feeling bad about the last thing. This stops us from fully immersing ourselves in what we're doing, and we end up skimming along at the surface level.

When we live out a one-dimensional, guilt-ridden definition of motherhood, we are bound to be grumpy. The present can't hold our attention because we aren't content with it—we are constantly wanting more. Our assumption that we can only get rid of our guilt if we fix the situation, combined with our assumption that the problem can only be solved in some mythical future, means that the present can feel useless to us. The only way to stop the guilt (and the distraction that comes with it) is to decide that the present is valuable—not once I get myself cleaned up, but right this minute. If we can do that, we can be content about time well spent and focus on the present.

The reality is that when I'm truly present, I love my life. I don't want to be anywhere else. I'm full of gratitude. I'm content. And the mundane things don't feel so . . . well, mundane. But this decision to remain rooted in the present is one we have to make over and over, because the future keeps tugging at us. We have to be vigilant in being present.

Let me give you a small example: the phone. Oy. It really is the beast I'm trying to tame. I decided that the first full hour after the girls wake up in the morning and the first full hour after nap time or school are no-phone times. I'd love to say that I do this all the time when they're awake, but at least two solid hours a day is a good start.

I've been trying this for eight months now, and I've found that on the days I'm faithful about doing it, I tend to go longer than an hour. I love what's happening so much that the phone loses some of its pull. The other thing I've noticed is that my girls aren't so needy afterward. Their tank is full. If I need to take a call, they are more likely to play happily without need-ing momma. Happy kids, happy mom, no?

We can't expect every moment with our kids to be perfect. They need to see us work hard, and they need to know they aren't the center of our universe. But we also need to be inten-tional about building relationships with them and speaking into their lives. If this sounds impossible, I encourage you to start small—maybe thirty minutes at first. Getting started is the hardest part—I truly believe you will see fruit soon. And before long, your focus muscle will grow, and you'll be able to escape the guilt cycle.

BECOMING A THIRTY-SOMETHING-YEAR-OLD STUDENT

One day after Vivi made Vana cry one too many times, I told Vivi to start watching her little sister's face. Vivi loves it when I give her responsibility and a special challenge. (Apparently playing with toys can get a little boring, even to a preschooler.) I told her that she could detect if Vana likes something she's doing by watching the expression she makes. Whether she's happy or about to start wailing, it's written all over her face.

As I coached Vivi about understanding her sister better, I couldn't help but think, *I want to become a student of my kids too.* It seemed almost magical. I love learning, and it sounded refreshing to have the opportunity to study and use my brain. I seek stimulation beyond coloring or playing airplane or mak-ing silly faces, and usually that quest for knowledge takes me away from my kids. I distract myself from being present with them through podcasts, Instagram, or text messages. But what if my stimulation actually came through interacting with my kids? What if I could stare into their faces and notice unique things about them?

God has given us the sacred responsibility of stewarding our kids. Maybe we'd enjoy them more if we knew we are called to do far more than just keep them alive. I know we mean it mostly as a joke: "Hey, I'm just doing what I can to keep them alive!" But thoughts are powerful. When our kids become adults, we are hoping they'll be more than just human beings who are still breathing. We want kids who have values instilled deep inside them. And when we recognize that our job as moms has lasting significance, it makes a difference in our energy level too. I find myself energized when I proactively try to instill good things in my kids. In contrast, my energy is depleted when I feel like my job is simply to be a milk machine or a diaper genie.

As I started to study my girls, I was surprised by how many new things I noticed. For example, when I lay Vana in her crib, if she stretches out her right arm, she's happy to have the space—she's done cuddling and ready to sleep. If she doesn't, a cry is coming. *When did this routine start?* I wondered. *How long has it taken me to notice this quirk of hers?* I feel a more intimate connection with her now that I've made this discovery. It has made me a better mom to Vana, and it has made me want to study my girls even more.

CLOSE THE LOOPS

Okay. It's time to get really practical. One of the biggest things that causes mental distraction is having too much unfinished business.

I'm sure you know the feeling: your brain is virtually ping-ponging from something you need to add to the grocery list to someone you forgot to text back to a question you want to ask your husband to something you need to google. Your mind never lands on one thing for more than a second or two before shooting off to the next thing.

When we have a mental loop open, it trips us up and distracts us from what's happening around us. When the ends start slapping us in the face, it's time to get serious about closing the loop.

I recently declared a "close the loop" day. If you'd like to try this too, here are some examples of what I tackled:

1. **Things I keep procrastinating about and have been talking or thinking about for days, weeks, or even months.** If you've spent hours over the last few months thinking about that ten-minute job you're dreading, it's time to tackle it and stop letting it eat away at your time.

2. **Things that will take five to ten minutes to complete.** Perhaps you have some five-minute tasks that you keep putting off, and now they're taking up a disproportionate amount of your brain space. Commit to knocking them all out at a certain time. A big one for me in this category is responding to text messages. I am terrible at this. In my mind, it will only take a second to respond, so I don't devote any big chunks of time to this task. I assume I'll fit it into the cracks. But usually my girls are present in the cracks, so not surprisingly, I find myself distracted, and my friends are left hanging.

3. **Things I need to let go of completely.** Have you been looking for a new comforter online for weeks? Is this something you really want to spend the money on now anyway? This was me recently. My constant

searching ate up time and brain space. It meant that I spent several evenings clicking around on my laptop instead of refreshing my mind for another full day. As you look at the open loops in your life, be ruthless and see what you can close by taking it off the list completely.

PERMISSION TO LIVE QUIETLY

I recently stumbled on this verse: "Aspire to live quietly, and to mind your own affairs, and to work with your hands, as we instructed you" (1 Thessalonians 4:11, ESV), and it seems especially appropriate for moms. It doesn't make specific mention of being present with our kids, but I feel like the Bible is giving me explicit permission to slow down. It's giving me permission not to be so tightly wound, ready to fix everything around me. It's giving me permission to tend to my own life and my own family. Yes, we're supposed to work hard, but I'm pretty sure the work Paul is talking about is less than what I usually try to cram onto my plate.

I loved watching *Downton Abbey* for the simple reason that it seemed a slower pace of life. That whole idea of having dinner and then retiring to the parlor for tea and chess sure sounds nice compared to the scramble around our house to clean dishes, give baths, pay bills online, and get ready for the next day. I realize they had a staff and all, but I love how they seemed to be in this cocoon that created the perfect setting for living in the present.

The noise of the world can perpetuate the lie that we will never be able to live undistracted. Times have changed. Technology is too much. Those were the old days. As I read E. M. Bounds's book *Purpose in Prayer*, I was reminded that all eras have their own distractions. Before 1913, Bounds had the nerve to say, "This is not a praying age; it is an age of great activity, of great movements, but one in which the tendency is very strong to stress the seen and the material, and to neglect and discount the unseen and the spiritual."[3] Bounds also tells the story of a man named James Gilmour, who "made a rule that when he got to the bottom of any page he would wait until the ink dried and spend the time in prayer."[4] In that day, it was common to use a blotter when writing so you didn't have to wait to keep going on the next page. The blotter: the 1900s version of a productivity tool. More than a hundred years ago, people were faced with their own distractions, their own great activity that could keep them from being fully present.

We may not change our blotter habits (because I'm guessing you don't have a blotter), but how can we apply this lesson to our own lives? Are there things we use to make our lives more efficient that we need to take a break from in order to embrace the quiet moments right in front of us? What's our version of praying until the ink dries?

Maybe for me this means sitting on Vivi's bed for another one of her meandering unicorn stories instead of jumping up to add something to my to-do list. Maybe it means drying your clothes on a clothesline so you can slow down and enjoy God's creation instead of tossing a load in the dryer before you run out the door. Maybe it means skipping the self-checkout and making meaningful conversation with a weary cashier. As these choices force us to slow down, we can't help but see what's in front of us instead of merely whizzing through our day.

When I'm able to slow down, I'm more aware of my tendency to become Grumpy Mom and can more effectively keep her at bay.

ACTION STEPS

1. **Be a student of your kids.** How can you use the information you observe about them to be a better parent? How can you simply enjoy knowing these things?

2. **Get a landline.** My phone is by far the biggest reason I don't connect with my kids as much as I'd like to, so we decided to get a landline. This allows me to tuck my phone away for the afternoon without convincing myself I *need* my phone in case there's an emergency. Only a handful of people have our home phone number, so the entire world can't reach me at any given moment.

3. **Designate "present time."** Even if you can't get a landline, find ways to unplug. In our house, the first hour after the girls wake up and the first hour after nap time is no-phone time.

4. **Commit to spending intentional time with your kids every day.** You don't have to do monumental things to be present with your kids. I find that I am most engaged with my girls when we have a book in our hands. You also might want to explain everyday activities to your kids, like cooking, gardening, or even folding clothes.

KEY VERSE

Make it your goal to live a quiet life, minding your own business and working with your hands.

1 THESSALONIANS 4:11

PRAYER

Lord, my heart wanders constantly to things that don't matter. I long to give my kids the attention they deserve, but instead I pick up my phone to see what someone I may never have met is doing. Teach me to be present with my family. Remove from my thoughts everything that competes with what you want me to settle my mind on in that moment. Show me how to have fun with my kids and how to make our time together fruitful. When they look back on their childhoods, may they remember my eyes and not my phone. In Jesus' name, amen.

Chapter 20

WE TURNED OUT AMAZING

Say Hello to Leaving a Legacy

WHEN PEOPLE TALK ABOUT the good ol' days, an inevitable sentiment comes up: "We turned out fine!" It sounds pretty harmless—and even a little funny in most cases. I remember being pregnant and turning down cold turkey, Caesar dressing with raw eggs, and other potential offenders I'd read I should avoid eating while pregnant. I can't tell you how many older mommas saw me skipping a chicken salad sandwich and thought I was going overboard.

"We turned out just fine, and our moms ate that while pregnant!" they'd say.

The advice doesn't just come in prenatal situations either.

"I had plenty of screen time as a kid, and I turned out fine."

"My parents left me to figure out what I believed on my own, and I turned out fine."

Mommas, "fine" is not our legacy. I'm not saying that if

you eat a turkey sandwich while pregnant that you don't care about your kids. I'm saying that we should aim higher than "just fine." God has called us to raise our little ones, and we should be eager to handle this stewardship with excellence. Our greatest responsibility is also one of our greatest blessings.

I know there are seasons when we just have to survive as moms (hello, first-trimester morning sickness and day four of the house-wide flu). There are times when we feed our kids chicken nuggets for several days running or plop them in front of the electronic babysitter. This is just part of life. But when I look at the overarching picture of raising my kids, I want these times to be the exception, not the rule.

Every night when I pray with Vivi and Vana, I let them hear me thank God that I get to be their mom. This is a role I don't take lightly. I don't want to spend the next decade and a half nurturing their souls to "just fine." I long for them to embrace the abundant life God has for them, and I don't know how they will do that if they see me handling one of my greatest callings with a "just fine" attitude.

We are one of the greatest, if not *the* greatest, influences in our kids' lives. This is exciting, right? But if I'm honest, sometimes I feel like legacies can wait. Dinner has a deadline, and that work project has a deadline. Your legacy may have a deadline too, but it's not a known deadline, and because of that, it's hard to make it a priority over the urgent things. By the time the dishes are done and the clothes are folded, there's little time left to form a legacy. So we put it off.

Our legacy matters—first and foremost because Jesus matters. As I think about everything I want to pass on to my kids, it all boils down to Jesus. I want my entire life to point them to him—including the mistakes I make and the way he transforms me. I'm not perfect at this mom thing, so when I inevitably make mistakes, I pray they'll see how much we all need Jesus.

This verse about legacy captures what I want to pass down generationally to my kids: "I am reminded of your sincere faith, which first lived in your grandmother Lois and in your mother Eunice and, I am persuaded, now lives in you also" (2 Timothy 1:5, NIV). I'm over here "amening" as I think about how much I'd love to leave a legacy like this.

If you feel weary thinking about having to do one more thing, remember that we have a role to play in this, but God is doing the heavy lifting. We just get to come alongside him in the work he's already doing.

WHO WILL THEY REMEMBER?

What do you want your kids to remember about their childhood? I hope mine will remember zoo days and turning the hearth in our living room into a stage. I hope they'll remember me saying "You can never lose my love!" and telling them all the things I love about them as I tuck them in at night. I hope they'll remember getting grace when they were supposed to get a consequence. And oh, I hope they'll remember the laughter we shared.

But there are also a lot of moments we hope our kids will forget. When I ask moms what they're afraid their legacy will be, the resounding answer is that their kids will remember a mom who is angry and constantly yelling.

Vivi is my "mini me" when it comes to personality. She's cautious and a rule follower, and sometimes I worry she'll take both of these traits too far, like I do sometimes, turning them into worry and legalism. There's something about having children that serves as a mirror for the soul. We know our kids aren't perfect, but it's sobering to think about the negative traits they might pick up from us.

As we talk about leaving a legacy and the qualities we want to instill in our kids, we need to start in a challenging spot: our own character. Deuteronomy 6:8 says, "Write these commandments that I've given you today on your hearts. Get them inside of you and then get them inside your children. Talk about them wherever you are, sitting at home or walking in the street; talk about them from the time you get up in the morning to when you fall into bed at night" (MSG). Did you catch that? The legacy we leave starts *inside* of us. I'm a doer, but lately I've been learning a lot about *not* doing. Even more important is who I am becoming. My legacy isn't simply about what I teach my kids; it's about who they see I am.

I've been guilty of teaching really good things to my kids but not holding myself to the same standard. I set a high standard for my children because I see why this is in their best interest, but when it comes to my own life, I seem to value myself less. John Ortberg says, "Because my inner life is invisible, it is easy to neglect. No one has direct access to it, so it wins no applause."[1] Maybe this is why we neglect soul-level change for ourselves. This kind of change is hard to measure, and no one is cheering us on.

Can we change that second part? My hope is that these last few pages will cheer you on in your pursuit of tending to your soul and being changed by God.

- There may be no applause when you learn not to respond immediately in fear, but your kids will experience the calm.

- There may be no applause when your grumpy mood lasts only a few minutes instead of all afternoon, but your kids will feel the new joy in your home.
- There may be no applause when you rely on Jesus instead of coffee first thing in the morning, but your kids will learn about dependence on the Lord.

I'm excited to see how a world of changed mommas will change their children and grandchildren as these future generations witness the kind of transformation that is possible only because of Jesus. I know change takes work, but I'm tired of doing the same thing over and over again and getting the same results.

- I'm tired of being a predictable mess when my husband comes home.
- I'm tired of yelling and getting angry so quickly.
- I'm tired of letting life toss me around.
- I'm tired of fearing every life stage for my kids.
- I'm ready for a legacy that comes only when I allow the Lord to transform my innermost being and gives me the wisdom to cultivate my children's hearts.

Fortunately, we aren't solely responsible for this kind of change. If it were solely up to me to create a lasting legacy, my kids wouldn't have a shot. But ultimately they are in God's hands, not mine. I'm just a steward, not the owner. I've released control, trusting that God, in his awesome power and love, cares for every detail of their lives.

And because of his power, it's possible for us to leave a legacy that's more than just "fine."

I want to pass down a joy that can't be stolen by unchecked emotions or seemingly bad days.

I want to pass down the value that the people around you matter more than your virtual following.

I want to pass down a sense of wonder and awe because I took time to actually notice God's creation.

I want my kids to remember a childhood that was more than just "fine" and a momma who was more than just grumpy.

I surely can't do all this on my own, but that's fitting, because I also want to pass down an unrelenting belief that we can't do this life apart from Jesus.

ACTION STEPS

1. **Talk to a mom a generation ahead of you.** Ask her about the legacy she has left behind. What is she glad she did as a mom, and what does she wish she'd done differently?

2. **Create a family vision.** Aim for more than "just fine." Get intentional about the values you want to instill in your family, and make a list of practical steps you can take to incorporate these values into your days.

3. **Pray for your kids.** Cover every aspect of your children's lives in prayer, believing that God has heard your heart's cry for them and that even if he has something different in mind from what you'd choose, his plans are good.

KEY VERSE

Write these commandments that I've given you today on your hearts. Get them inside of you and then get them inside your children. Talk about them wherever you are, sitting at home or walking in the street; talk about them from the time you get up in the morning to when you fall into bed at night.

DEUTERONOMY 6:8, MSG

PRAYER

Father, thank you for choosing me to be the mom for my kids. What a blessing you've bestowed on me! Show me how to steward their hearts well. Please make me aware of every opportunity to point them to you. Give me courage to say I'm sorry when I'm wrong so I can model forgiveness and grace to them. And please pour out your grace on me when I don't influence them well. In Jesus' name, amen.

EPILOGUE

I'M PRETTY SURE YOU KNOW by now that this book is written not by an expert but by a "journeywoman," as my friend Hunter Beless would say. These are concepts I'm preaching to myself most of all.

I remember the moment I realized that these truths are changing me—that although Grumpy Mom still camps out in my heart at times, she no longer has permanent residence. I was lying in bed after a long Sunday. It started out with a toddler puking, juuust to give you the lay of the land. I was leaving town in less than forty-eight hours for a huge event for Val Marie Paper. There was still a ton to do, and normally the news that I'd have a sick kid home from school the next day would have sent me straight into Grumpy Mom mode, wishing I could escape my life and feeling sorry for myself about how hard things were.

But that day was different. I was steady. I worked hard. I took care of Vivi. I didn't complain. And this wasn't phony. Believe me when I say I have no poker face.

No, the steadiness I felt was because I was finally starting to believe the truth instead of the lies we've spent the past 239 pages talking about. The truth is taking root, my moments of crying in the bathroom are dwindling, and my moments of enjoying motherhood, even on the really hard days, are increasing.

Just last night, under her fluffy flamingo blanket, Vivi told me, "Momma, you're a different momma."

First, I made sure she meant this in a positive way, because you know kids. They shoot straight. (I know this because lately she has asked way too many ladies if they had a baby in their belly when, in fact, they did not.) When she confirmed that she meant this in a positive way, I almost cried.

Here was the scene from moments earlier: I asked her to clean up her toys, and she challenged my authority. I got down on her level and spoke calmly and quietly to her, with lots of grace. The situation was resolved with a hug and no hard feelings on either side. I promise you this has not been my first response in the past, but all this truth has been sinking in, and it's changing everything.

This is my hope for you, too, momma. I want this for us—not just because I want us to be happy. Yes, I care about your happiness, but there's an even deeper goal than that. God has been so gracious to give us abundant life here on earth, and it's devastating to think we'd waste that because we're too tuned in to the world. He's saying to us, "Look! This is what I have for you in motherhood!" while we're distracted by yoga pants and complaining about the carpool line.

Maybe you picked up this book *hoping* for change but not

really believing it could happen for you. It can, and I'm living proof. (I spared you the exclamation points right there so it wouldn't seem like an infomercial promising you the world, but this is big, y'all.) If anyone was cut out for being forever stuck in Grumpy Mom land, it was me. If I can do it, I know you can too.

So let's keep rejecting the lies and holding on to the truth. God has made a life of freedom available to us.

> It wasn't so long ago that you were mired in that old stagnant life of sin. You let the world, which doesn't know the first thing about living, tell you how to live. You filled your lungs with polluted unbelief, and then exhaled disobedience. We all did it, all of us doing what we felt like doing, when we felt like doing it, all of us in the same boat. It's a wonder God didn't lose his temper and do away with the whole lot of us. Instead, immense in mercy and with an incredible love, he embraced us. He took our sin-dead lives and made us alive in Christ. He did all this on his own, with no help from us! . . . God does both the making and saving. He creates each of us by Christ Jesus to join him in the work he does, the good work he has gotten ready for us to do, work we had better be doing.
> EPHESIANS 2:1-10, MSG

We have been freed from living that old stagnant life of sin and bondage. We are free from the limits the world puts on motherhood. We are now under the authority of God, and that includes living out a more abundant motherhood.

We don't have to wait for a kid-free vacation to experience soul-level refreshment.

We don't have to wait for nap time to find joy.

We don't have to wait until our kids leave the house to fulfill our callings.

So this is goodbye, Grumpy Mom. Time to pack your bags. We'll be just fine here without you.

ACKNOWLEDGMENTS

TYLER: THANK YOU FOR NOT laughing too hard when I decided to write this book. You've probably sacrificed more to make this book happen than I have. Thank you for reminding me each time mommy guilt crept in why I was writing this book. You pushed me not only to write this but to enjoy the process, and I will never forget that!

Vivi and Vana, my sweet girls: I thank God every day that he entrusted me with being your momma. I'm grateful for your patience as I learn to live more moments without Grumpy Mom and for your willingness to share your momma's attention with this book-baby.

Natalie: I can't wait to see the mom you become one day, and I hope this book will save you many of the Grumpy Mom moments you witnessed from me!

Mom and Dad: Is it possible to love you two even more, watching you as grandparents to our girls? No words can express how lucky I am to have y'all as parents—and only four doors down.

Mimi: I hit the mother-in-law jackpot with you. I cannot tell you how many times I've thanked God for your presence in my life and our girls' lives. You raised my best friend, and for that I'm eternally grateful.

Kara and Ashley: You were two of the best decisions I've ever made with Val Marie Paper. When people were surprised that I was able to balance Val Marie Paper and writing a book, I would simply giggle and thank God for you two.

To the Val Marie Paper community: Thank you for joining me on this journey. I didn't write this book in a vacuum. It felt like a conversation I've long wanted to have with each momma who has read one of my momma posts and said, "This is just what I needed today!" We are in this together, and I am grateful to finally encourage you with more than the character limit will allow—even if it does mean fewer emojis!

Thank you, Gretchen Saffles and Michelle Myers. I have loved walking this journey of being shop owners with y'all. I always leave our conversations grateful that we have each other and inspired to keep working for God's Kingdom, not mine.

Thank you, Jennifer Dukes Lee, for going before me and cheering me on. I felt like I had an expert big sister in my corner, and I've always been so humbled by every word you've said about me.

Thank you, Diana Kerr. I knew when I went into the writing season that I'd need someone to help me navigate this season well. Any author would be lucky to call you their life coach. I'm glad to call you my friend, too.

Thank you, Mrs. Duke, for instilling in me such a love for words. Your belief in me gave me the confidence to believe I could be a writer.

Thank you, Sarah, for casually asking me at the pool one day if I had another book in me. I said I had an idea for a book on motherhood but wasn't sure I could really write it. That question sparked something in me and encouraged this idea to take shape. Thank you!

Thank you, Claudia Cross, for helping me make sense of a world I knew nothing about and for willingly taking on all the logistics of publishing so I could focus on "the fun stuff" and on writing a book I'm proud of.

Thank you, Tyndale team! I have never felt so supported by a company. That's because it's not just a name but people who have truly cared about me through every step of this process. Kara, thank you for finding me. Your confidence in me impacted this project more than you'll know. Thank you, Sarah, for your excitement and energy. I'm not sure many authors can say their publisher flew in to have a hamburger and shake with them! And I never imagined publisher calls could contain so much laughter. Stephanie, I now want you to edit all my written words. Let's be safe and include text messages, too, because you refine my rough ideas and do so in the most encouraging way. Julie, thank you for taking my concept and creating a design that a picky designer is forever grateful will accompany many a momma during nap time or in the carpool line!

Thank you to every momma-friend in my life who has made me believe that we are more than just dirty hair and yoga pants. You sparked a hope that this melancholy gal could cling to for dear life on the hard days.

NOTES

CHAPTER 1: EMOJI OVERLOAD
1. Peter Scazzero, *Emotionally Healthy Spirituality: It's Impossible to Be Spiritually Mature while Remaining Emotionally Immature* (Grand Rapids, MI: Zondervan, 2006), 49–50.
2. Elisabeth Elliot, *Discipline: The Glad Surrender* (Grand Rapids, MI: Fleming H. Revell, 2006), 71.

CHAPTER 3: GIVE ME ALL THE MASSAGES
1. John Ortberg, *Soul Keeping: Caring for the Most Important Part of You* (Grand Rapids, MI: Zondervan, 2014), 172.
2. Matthew Henry's Commentary, *BibleGateway*, https://www.bible gateway.com/resources/matthew-henry/Mark.13.28-Mark.13.37.

CHAPTER 4: HANDS ON LIKE A HELICOPTER
1. Nancy Groom, *From Bondage to Bonding: Escaping Codependency, Embracing Biblical Love* (Colorado Springs: NavPress, 1991), 47.
2. Max Lucado, *Anxious for Nothing: Finding Calm in a Chaotic World* (Nashville: Thomas Nelson, 2017), 4.

CHAPTER 6: WHEN THEY CRY, I EAT CHOCOLATE
1. Darren Hardy, *The Compound Effect: Jumpstart Your Income, Your Life, Your Success* (New York: Vanguard, 2010), 83.

CHAPTER 7: ON EMPTY
1. Elisabeth Elliot, *Discipline: The Glad Surrender* (Grand Rapids, MI: Fleming H. Revell, 2006), 70.
2. E. M. Bounds, *E. M. Bounds on Prayer* (New Kensington, PA: Whitaker House, 1997), 37–38.
3. Valerie Woerner, *The Finishing School* (CreateSpace, 2015), 177.

CHAPTER 8: WHAT'S NEXT, PAPA?

1. Elisabeth Elliot, *Discipline: The Glad Surrender* (Grand Rapids, MI: Fleming H. Revell, 2006), 35.

CHAPTER 9: ROUGH EDGES

1. Lara Casey, *Cultivate: A Grace-Filled Guide to Growing an Intentional Life* (Nashville: W Publishing, 2017), 49.

CHAPTER 11: IT'S TEMPORARY

1. Chip and Joanna Gaines, *The Magnolia Story*, with Mark Dagostino (Nashville, W Publishing, 2016), 53.
2. Jim Loehr and Tony Schwartz, *The Power of Full Engagement: Managing Energy, Not Time, Is the Key to High Performance and Personal Renewal* (New York: The Free Press, 2003), 13, 29.
3. Lara Casey, *Cultivate: A Grace-Filled Guide to Growing an Intentional Life* (Nashville: W Publishing, 2017), 52.

CHAPTER 12: LIGHTEN YOUR LOAD

1. *Friends' Intelligencer*, vol. 18 (Philadelphia: T. Ellwood Zell, 1862), 195.
2. Elisabeth Elliot, *Discipline: The Glad Surrender* (Grand Rapids, MI: Fleming H. Revell, 2006), 99.

CHAPTER 13: THE NOT-SO-QUIET TIME

1. Saundra Dalton-Smith, *Sacred Rest* (New York: FaithWords, 2017), 136.
2. Darren Hardy, *The Compound Effect: Jumpstart Your Income, Your Life, Your Success* (New York: Vanguard, 2010), 105–106.
3. E. M. Bounds, *E. M. Bounds on Prayer* (New Kensington, PA: Whitaker House, 1997), 69.

CHAPTER 14: ROLE CALL

1. Mark and Susan Merrill, *Lists to Love By for Busy Wives* (New York: FaithWords, 2017), 21.

CHAPTER 15: PLAYS WELL WITH OTHERS

1. Dietrich Bonhoeffer, *Life Together: A Discussion of Christian Fellowship* (New York: Harper & Row, 1954), 18.
2. Ibid., 27.
3. Ibid., 19.
4. Jennifer Dukes Lee, *The Happiness Dare* (Carol Stream, IL: Tyndale House, 2016), 48.
5. Elisabeth Elliot, *Discipline: The Glad Surrender* (Grand Rapids, MI: Fleming H. Revell, 2006), 63.

CHAPTER 16: AN OPEN LETTER AGAINST OPEN LETTERS

1. John Bevere, *The Bait of Satan* (Lake Mary, FL: Charisma House, 1994), 8.
2. Gordon MacDonald, *Ordering Your Private World* (Nashville: Thomas Nelson, 2003), 146.

CHAPTER 17: OTHER MOMMIES MADE ME DO IT

1. Joshua Becker, "The Life-Giving Benefits of Owning Less" (sermon, Grace Chapel, Lincoln, NE, December 4, 2016), http://www.gracepca .com/sermons/2016/12/4/the-life-giving-benefits-of-owning-less-12-04 -2016.
2. Hannah Anderson, *Humble Roots: How Humility Grounds and Nourishes Your Soul* (Chicago: Moody Publishers, 2016), 42.
3. Peter Scazzero, *Emotionally Healthy Spirituality: Unleash a Revolution in Your Life in Christ* (Nashville: Thomas Nelson, 2006), 147.
4. "Decision Fatigue," *Wikipedia.org*, https://en.wikipedia.org/wiki /Decision_fatigue.
5. Becker, "Owning Less."
6. Elisabeth Elliot, *Discipline: The Glad Surrender* (Grand Rapids, MI: Fleming H. Revell, 2006), 146.

CHAPTER 18: PUT YOUR SHOES ON!

1. Mark Buchanan, *The Rest of God: Restoring Your Soul by Restoring Sabbath* (Nashville: Thomas Nelson, 2006), 45.
2. Shauna Niequist, *Present Over Perfect: Leaving behind Frantic for a Simpler, More Soulful Way of Living* (Grand Rapids, MI: Zondervan, 2016), 45.
3. Mark E. Thibodeaux, *Reimagining the Ignatian Examen: Fresh Ways to Pray from Your Day* (Chicago: Loyola Press, 2015), x–xi.

CHAPTER 19: GETTING MOMMA'S ATTENTION

1. Michelle Myers, *Famous in Heaven and at Home: A 31-Day Character Study of the Proverbs 31 Woman* (Myers Cross Training, 2016), 237–38.
2. Peter Scazzero, *Emotionally Healthy Spirituality: Unleash a Revolution in Your Life in Christ* (Nashville: Thomas Nelson, 2006), 80–81.
3. E. M. Bounds, *Purpose in Prayer* (New Kensington, PA: Whitaker House, 1997), 52.
4. Ibid., 47.

CHAPTER 20: WE TURNED OUT AMAZING

1. John Ortberg, *Soul Keeping: Caring for the Most Important Part of You* (Grand Rapids, MI: Zondervan, 2014), 38.

ABOUT THE AUTHOR

 VALERIE WOERNER is an author and the owner of Val Marie Paper, where her mission is to create practical tools and content that equip women to cut through the noise of everyday life and find fullness in the presence of the Lord.

Before starting Val Marie Paper in 2012, Valerie owned a wedding planning business and fell in love with paper design while creating wedding invitations for clients. During her first pregnancy, she created a prayer journal that she desperately needed—and she quickly found that many other women needed it too!

She graduated from Louisiana Tech University in 2007 with a degree in journalism and English. She thought she was destined to work for a big magazine in New York City but found she enjoyed personal column writing more. Her experience designing newspaper pages and her love for writing have come full circle, as she uses both to create content and products that encourage women to transform their lives through prayer and action.

Valerie lives in Lafayette, Louisiana, with her husband, Tyler, and their two daughters, Vivi and Vana. She loves reading, going on barefoot walks around her neighborhood, taking Sunday naps on her screened-in porch, and eating good Cajun food.

You can visit Valerie's shop at http://www.valmariepaper.com.

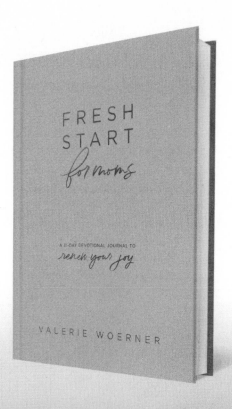

VAL MARIE PAPER

where prayer meets practical